KAZAKHSTAN'S DYNAMIC ECONOMY:

A Business and Investment Review

Series editor: Dr Marat Terterov

GMB

Publisher's note

GMB Publishing Ltd.
120 Pentonville Road
London N1 9JN
United Kingdom
www.globalmarketbriefings.com

This edition first published 2007 by GMB Publishing Ltd.

Hardcopy ISBN 1-84673-010-4 E-report ISBN 1-84673-011-2

British Library Cataloguing in Publication Data

A CIP record for this book is available from the British Library

Contents

About the Authors

Salans

Almaty is a leading full-service international law firm with more than 25 years of experience in the Commonwealth of Independent States. In Kazhakstan they combine the expertise and resources of a large international practice with personal local knowledge from partners who are sensitive to the business, legal and cultural nuances of the region. Their dedication, excellence, integrity and responsiveness allow them to consistently provide a high-quality legal service and advice.

Almaty
Salans LLP
135 Aylai Khan Avenue
Almaty, Kazakhstan
050000
Tel: (732) 7258 2380
Fax: (732) 7258 2381
e-mail: almaty@salans.com

Atyrau
55 Aiteke Bi St. Suite 2103
River Palace Hotel, 1st floor
Atyrau, Kazakhstan
060011
Tel: (731) 2297 0040 or 2297 0041
Fax: (731) 2297 0042
e-mail: atyrau@salans.com
www.salans.com

Dr Marat Terterov

Dr Terterov is a comparative specialist and regional expert focusing on Russia/former-Soviet states and the Middle East. His experience has been acquired during nearly 10 year of work in academia, government, private sector and international development consulting. Playing the role of a pro-active analyst and being employed by a wide range of organizations, Dr Terterov specializes in the provision of in-depth economic and political research, public policy evaluation, non-financial corporate due diligence and investment promotion services. A highly insightful and original commentator, he holds a PhD in the political-economy of the Middle East from Oxford University and has published over 40 articles and books on a diversity of economic, political and business topics relating to the Middle East and Russia-ex-Soviet Union.

At the present time (summer 2006) Dr Terterov holds two permanent employment positions: Foreign Policy Specialist on Russian-Eurasian relations with the Persian Gulf States at the Gulf Research Centre Think Tank in Dubai, United Arab Emirates; and Conference Director for Russian Energy at C5/Euroforum, an information management and events production company based in London. He also provides ongoing consulting services to a range of corporate clients. His most recent projects involve in-depth analysis of the Russian natural gas industry, primarily focusing on Gazprom, the Russian gas monopoly and the world's largest producer of natural gas. Dr Terterov is an Australian national, speaks English, Russian and is conversant in Egyptian Arabic. He has lived and worked in a diversity of countries throughout Europe, North America, the Middle East and Russia-ex-Soviet Union and is deeply familiar with the cultures of both East and West.

Douglas Townsend

Douglas Townsend Consulting.
Honorary Consul of the Republic of Kazakhstan in Wales.
Former Australian Ambassador to the Republic of Kazakhstan.

Townsend is a UK-based business consultant specialising in trade and investment with markets in the CIS and CEE countries. He writes and edits economic publications and presents at economic conferences dealing with these regions, in which he regularly travels.

Townsend is Senior Adviser to the International Tax & Investment Center, Washington (also Almaty, Astana, Baku, Kiev, Moscow, London); Secretary to the Caspian Minerals Tax Committee, Houston (also London & Moscow); and Director of the Kazakhstan Minerals Taxation Academy, Astana and Azerbaijan Minerals Taxation Academy, Baku.

A Council member of the British-Kazakh Society, he participates in the DTI-supported KBTIC (Kazakhstan British Trade & Investment Council) and CATBIG (Central Asia Turkey Business Information Group). He is also a member of the Anglo-Azerbaijan Society, the British Association for Central & Eastern Europe and the Royal Institute of International Affairs.

Formerly, Townsend was Australian Ambassador (Kazakhstan, Hungary, Switzerland, Senegal, Cote d'Ivoire); Australian Investment Commissioner Europe (Germany-based); and Australian WMD disarmament negotiator (Canberra, Vienna). He also served in Australian diplomatic missions in Pakistan, Ireland and Vietnam.

Resident in Wales, Townsend is a life member of the Royal Welsh Agricultural Society and member of the Institute of Welsh Affairs and of the Friends of the University of Wales, Lampeter.

Contact: E-dat.temas@btinternet.com; M-07768 091901; T-01570 423403.

Preface

The Republic of Kazakhstan continued to assert itself as a dynamic transitional economy and attractive emerging market during 2005. The country's economy grew by 9.4 per cent in 2004 and the strong economic performance continued during 2005. Much of the country's economic expansion continued as a result of increased oil and gas production, with oil and gas condensate output rising by 4.7 per cent during January–October 2005. With global demand for energy rising inexorably, the performance of the country's energy sector only served to reinforce Kazakhstan's importance as a major energy supplying country. The republic continues to be the source of substantial interest from international energy companies, many who have made major investments in Kazakhstan since its independence.

However, the energy sector is not the only source of investor interest in this major Eurasian country; numerous other large-scale industrial investment projects are being implemented. In fact, several hundred investments valued at over US $1.5 billion, many of which have foreign holdings, are currently underway. Amongst the most important of these are investments in the production of Skoda automobiles, Kamaz vehicles and other transport production projects.

The republic's continued and widely recognized regional leadership in both economic and political reform has further aided Kazakhstan's ability to develop economically. During December 2005, Kazakhstan's long-serving president, Nursultan Nazerbayev, was re-elected for a subsequent presidential term in an election, which a number of foreign observers rate as surprisingly competitive. While Kazakhstan's democratic institutions are still emerging, the presence of President Nazerbayev continues to create a strong semblance of political stability in the country, which is vital for attracting investment and facilitating growth. Although further reforms are necessary to enhance the country's business environment and attract more investment into vital sectors, Kazakhstan continues to nurture its reputation internationally as a dynamic economy in the fast–growing, strategic Caspian region, as well as a major energy supplier to the international economy.

Guest author's introduction: Kazakhstan's political economy

Douglas Townsend Consulting, Former Australian Ambassador to Kazakhstan

Since the 2004 edition of this publication, Kazakhstan has sustained its significant economic upswing such that gross domestic product (GDP) exceeded US $50 billion during 2005, with GDP per capita for this very large, resource-rich, but moderately populated (15.1 million people) country reaching some $3,000. In 2003, Kazakhstan had qualified as a 'market economy' under the terms set by the European Union (EU) and United States, and while large-scale privatization remains incomplete, the private sector is now very substantial, entrepreneurship is encouraged and business associations proliferate, prices continue to be liberalized and prudential regulation of the financial services sector instituted.

Over the last five years economic growth rates of 9.0–13.5 per cent have been achieved along with comparative stability in the Consumer Price Index (CPI), which has stayed in the 6–8 per cent band. This is due to the expansion of the petroleum sector (production currently exceeds one million barrels per day and is expected to at least double in the next decade) and favourable commodity prices. Net foreign direct investment (FDI) inflows, largely to the oil sector, jumped to $5.5 billion in 2004 before settling at $3 billion during 2005, with UK-origin investments commanding first place until last year. Official reserves, including the National Fund, have risen to a historic high of US $15.1 billion, the budget is essentially in balance, and Kazakhstan's investment rating remained the highest in the Commonwealth of Independent States (CIS) at BBB/BBB+.

The 'non-oil' economy, including sectors such as metals and metallurgy, construction, and grains and fibres has also grown strongly during the decade at 6–8 per cent annually overall and is contributing four-fifths of GDP. Capacity constraints could impede continuation of this rate of development although labour supply seems buoyed by significant immigration (much of it illegal) numbers. A greater concern, in the opinion of the International Finance Institutions (IFIs) and backed by the findings of the European Bank for Reconstruction and Development (EBRD)/World Bank 'BEEPS' Survey 2005, is perceived slackening in the pace of the transition to a genuine market economy. Hence the IFIs recommended reinvigorated structural reform to improve the investment climate and lower the cost of doing business in Kazakhstan, not least for domestic and foreign small-to-medium enterprises (SMEs). Subsequently the World Bank survey "Doing Business 2007" recorded a significant improvement, with Kazakhstan achieving 52nd place among 175 economies compared with 63rd place last year. The IFIs also recommended improving governance and in that respect the Kazakhstan Government and the country's major resources companies have adhered to the UK Government's Extractive Industries Transparency Initiative (EITI) since October 2005.

Kazakhstan has continued its integration into major global and regional markets, particularly for hydrocarbons. This is evident in significant new essential pipeline construction and associated export-related infrastructure, the financing of which has also been supported by international development banks. Metal and grain exports have flourished and some of Kazakhstan's major metals and finance companies have listed on the London Stock Exchange. Substantive regional integration in Eurasia/ Central Asia has moved a step closer with the development of the Single Economic Space (members: Belarus, Kazakhstan, Russia, Ukraine) and the Eurasia Economic Community (members: Belarus, Kazakhstan, Kyrgyzstan, Russia, Tajikistan, Uzbekistan. Armenia, Moldova, Ukraine observers) as well as the conclusion of bilateral free trade agreements with regional partners including Russia and China. Increasingly Kazakhstan sees its potential to play a stronger regional role, even as a 'springboard' to dealings with China as Beijing looks to its west; but its realization requires a sustained effort.

Since 2004, Kazakhstan has largely set the pace for democratization within the Eurasian region. The third, regular Majilis (lower house of Kazakhstan's parliament) election since Independence (held on 19 September 2004, with some run-off polls on 3rd October 2004) proved competitive, with over 700 candidates from 12 political parties plus independents competing directly for 77 parliamentary seats. The Organization for Security and Cooperation in Europe (OSCE) Expert Observer Mission was highly critical of the Election Law and its administration as falling below the standards of the OSCE Copenhagen Declaration 2000. However, the 50 per cent level of voter participation combined with the record number of candidates and political parties made it the most open and competitive poll in Kazakhstan's post-independence history, indicating the growth of a healthy pluralism in the Kazakhstan polity. The various party leaders who felt marginalized by the Election Law and its implementation nonetheless remained constructive in their criticism and confirmed their engagement with the parliamentary way in Kazakhstan. This was demonstrated in subsequent polls, despite foreign predictions of a 'colour revolution', as in some neighbouring jurisdictions.

On 19 August 2005 in elections to Kazakhstan's Senate (the upper chamber of the parliament) the pro-presidential Otan party scored an easy victory, winning 10 of the 32 elective mandates. Then on 4 December 2005, over 75 per cent of Kazahkstan's 8.6 million registered voters cast ballots at some 9,580 polling stations to re-elect President Nursultan Nazarbayev by the substantial margin of 90 per cent. This overwhelming result paradoxically understated the degree of legally sanctioned, organized opposition faced for the first time in a presidential election in Kazakhstan, with two of the other unsuccessful candidates being substantive, nationally known personalities. Broadly, the result was assessed as a vote against importing regional instability and for sustaining economic development.

While there were again shortcomings compared to Copenhagen standards, as documented by the OSCE Expert Observer Mission, the 2005 presidential election was a genuine competition and represented an important step forward, both for Kazakhstan and the entire region.

Important and positive amendments to the electoral law had been made in response to the 2004 recommendations of the OSCE. Compared to the 2004 Majilis election, there were significant improvements in the leadership and workings of the Central Election Commission (CEC), with greater transparency and responsiveness to complaints and inquiries. The election was a genuine contest and the large turnout confirmed that the Kazakh people believed their votes mattered in this election. Significantly, all the major candidates called for an extension of elective principles to sub-national levels. Based on this election, Kazakhstan's clear regional leadership on economic and social reform could continue with further political reforms.

When President Nazarbayev was sworn in for a new seven-year term, he echoed a number of the themes of the December 2005 presidential election campaign with his vision of continued economic growth, democratic reforms and greater stability and security, with Kazakhstan joining the ranks of the world's 50 most competitive nations in the medium-to-longer term. (In the WEF *Global Competitiveness Report 2006-2007 published in September 2006,* Kazakhstan scored 56th place among 125 economies analysed). This vision forms the cornerstone of his policies, designed to preserve inter-ethnic and religious accord, maintain political stability against a backdrop of genuine democratization and combat systemic threats to national security. He thus the State Committee on Democratization (foreshadowed in September 2005 in succession to the National Commission on Democratization and Self-Government, and boycotted since 2002 by the opposition) has been established under his chairmanship and has developed a detailed political reform program. Defeated Ak Zhol party presidential candidate Alikhan Baimenov indicated he will participate in the Democratization Committee and take up the Parliamentary mandate he secured in the 2004 legislative elections. Rival candidate Tuyakbai has also successfully launched the new Social Democratic Party of Kazakhstan.

The reform process has also encouraged a more forthright approach to all aspects of economic development by the Kazakh Parliament and its committees. De-centralising power will involve revising intergovernmental fiscal relations, with tricky questions of 'vertical' balance between levels of government and 'horizontal' fiscal parity between regions to be negotiated, whilst avoiding ethnic polarization and containing the influence of local oligarchs. With a change in the Presidency now in prospect although in the medium-to-longer term, it could be expected that the political arena would become more contested over time.

Key elements of the President's comprehensive programme, outlined in his 1st March 2006 "Address to the Nation" and confirmed in his speech when opening the Winter Session of the Parliament in September, include significant tax and tariff reforms; among other things, a flat individual income tax rate to 'stave off corruption and stimulate entrepreneurial activity'. Ensuring that exchange rates are flexible and inflation is kept in check are major macroeconomic objectives in an environment of sustained dramatic economic growth (annualized 8–9 per cent) with an official aim to double GDP in the period 2006–2008. Efforts have been intensified to energize the 'clusters'-based industrial policy 2004–2015, creating conditions for value-added business development around the oil and gas industries; for promotion of new development in selected economic growth sectors including agriculture and textiles (cotton), aerospace and ICT; and for establishing regional corporations to support social development and entrepreneurial activity. To this end, special economic zones and preferential tax regimes have been created.

Ambitions for Kazakh Prime Minister Danyal Akhmetov's Government include the following:

- buying into domestic and foreign 'start-up' companies developing new technologies of commercial value;
- recreating the Ex-Im Bank so that Kazakhstan can participate in syndicating export credits for major international projects;
- promoting Kazakhstan's exports with trademarks and intellectual property rights;
- creating a state holding company (based on the model of Singapore's Temasek), which would encompass the government's assets in 'the strategic industries' of oil and gas, telecommunications, railways and utilities;
- promoting Almaty as a major regional financial centre;
- developing infrastructure and services industries, including the establishment of an internationally competitive aviation industry in partnership with major international aerospace companies.

The state holding company Samruk (Phoenix), under the chairmanship of Sir Richard Evans (formerly BAE) with former Deputy Prime Minister and Minister of Industry, Sauat Mynbaev as CEO, has now been established. The City of London is closely involved with the development of the regional financial centre in Almaty and the United Kingdom is also one preferred partner for the mandated 'higher education' cooperation required by the envisaged 'knowledge-based' economy.

Although Kazakhstan has progressed negotiations on agriculture and services, fulfilling its plan to join the World Trade Organization (WTO) has required new legislation, which meets WTO requirements for standards and government procurement; reform of taxation and customs systems in the energy sector including the introduction of a transparent tax system for the internal fuel market; and elimination of limitations on foreign investors' participation in the financial, insurance and construction sectors. New intellectual property protection legislation has been one important step forward but the outstanding agenda remains significant and the responsible Trade and Industry Minister, Vladimir Shkolnik, has indicated that accession to the WTO is now more likely in 2007.

Kazakhstan is situated in a region of intense and diverse interest to a wide range of foreign powers, putting a premium on Astana's wise statecraft and diplomacy. According to President Nazarbayev, Kazakhstan's external security would be centred around it meeting its international commitments, including in the critical sphere of energy security. As stated in the President's "Address to the Nation" 1st March 2006 Kazakhstan remains committed to 'strategic partnership with Russia, China and the USA', expanding cooperation with the EU and Muslim countries and strengthening relations with its Central Asian neighbours. A recent, potentially powerful association for realizing some of this objective is the Shanghai Cooperation Organization (SCO-members include Kazakhstan, Russia, China and Uzbekistan, with observers from many other interested parties including India and Pakistan). The United

Kingdom and Kazakhstan agreed upon their own high-level 'strategic partnership' in 2002. Heightened economic cooperation is one critical way in which the potential of this partnership can be practically realized.

Kazakhstan's foreign investment climate

Diana Brett, Salans, Almaty

Reforms and progress

Since independence in 1991, Kazakhstan has made considerable progress towards the establishment of a market economy and an attractive climate for foreign investment. Nearly US $30 billion of FDI has poured into Kazakhstan's economy, primarily due to immense reserves in the natural and mineral resources sector and incentives for investors in other priority sectors.

The Government of Kazakhstan has adopted several programmes important to their relations with foreign investors. In May 2003, President Nazarbayev signed off two state programmes to determine the country's development trends until 2015. The strategy for industrial innovation development is tasked with diversifying the economy through the development of market economy principles. Kazakhstan hopes to abide by all EU standards by 2015. The financial sector is expected to comply fully by 2007. Capital inflows and commodity exports have allowed the National Bank of Kazakhstan (NBK) to accumulate foreign exchange reserves and lower interest rates as inflation remains under control.

In 2000, the EU recognized Kazakhstan's economic reforms and in 2002 the US Department of Commerce granted Kazakhstan market economy status. Over the past 14 years (aggressively for more than half that time), Kazakhstan's government has implemented liberal and extensive economic reforms and embarked upon large-scale privatization programmes.

However, for the past several years the government has increasingly tended to challenge investor contracts, legislate protections and preferences for local companies and operators, and overly legislate procurement activities and infrastructure privatizations. Ambiguous legislation and inconsistent policy implementations have resulted in the widespread belief that Kazakhstan is not as open to foreign investment as it was in the years immediately following independence (1992–1998).

Legislation

Foreign investors in Kazakhstan are impacted by five major pieces of legislation: the Law On Investments, 2003; the Law On State Procurement, 2002; the Tax Code, 2001; the Customs Code, 2003; and Rules on Employing Foreign Labor, 2001. These five laws are intended to provide for currency convertibility; guarantees for legislative stability; a system of transparent government procurement; a transparent process for hiring expatriate professional workers; and incentives for investments in priority sectors, including infrastructure, health and tourism (to date still underdeveloped in Kazakhstan.) Inconsistent implementation of these and other key laws remains a primary obstacle to doing business.

The Law On Investments

In January 2003, President Nazarbayev signed a new Law On Investments. This new law disposes of the previous Law On Foreign Investment (27 December 1994) and Law On State Support of Direct Investment (28 February 1997) formerly governing foreign investment. The new law seeks to establish a single investment regime for both domestic and foreign investors.

Although the Law On Investments provides for dispute settlement through negotiation, Kazakhstan's judicial system and international arbitration, it narrows down the definition of investment disputes and lacks clear mechanisms for access to international arbitration. Kazakhstan's Constitution as well as the Law On Investments specify that international agreements have precedence over domestic law.

The law includes investment incentives preferring government-determined priority activities providing for investment tax preferences, customs duties exemptions and in-kind grants exclusively to Kazakhstan legal entities. Under the law, the government may rescind these incentives and collect back payments on duties (with fines) if the investor fails to fulfill contractual obligations. Because the application process calls for a business plan, which can be largely based on speculation, virtually all projects could be subject to incentive removal. Something of note and importance for foreign investors is that the new law does provide exemptions for customs duties on imported equipment if locally produced stocks are not available or do not meet international standards.

Although the law allows nationalization of investments, it does not provide clear grounds for expropriation. The law differentiates between nationalization and requisition, providing full indemnification of the investor in the case of the former, but payment of market value only in the case of the latter. Contradictory norms hinder the legal system. In the event of a contradiction, there are definitions for which laws take precedence; yet stability clauses, granted under earlier investment laws to investors, do not necessarily protect investors from amendments or other legislative and tax changes. Kazakhstan will provide compensation for contract violations when the government has 'guaranteed' the contracts. In cases where the contract was merely 'approved' by the government its responsibility is limited to its administrative duty to facilitate the subject investment activity.

The Law on Government Procurement – petroleum sector procurement rules

Since 1997, the state has increasingly favoured domestic investors over foreigners in most state contracts. Amendments passed in 1999 for subsurface legislation require mining and oil companies to increase their use of domestically produced goods and local services. In 2002, regulations for the implementation of these provisions were enacted, but to date the government has not taken action to implement the decree.

The Tax Code

Effective since January 2002, the Tax Code applies taxes universally and allows only a finite set of exemptions. The code is based upon an international taxation model and is considered a vast improvement over previous versions with huge progress towards establishing a transparent tax system. Effective since 1 January 2004, amendments to the tax code included reducing value added tax (VAT) from 16 per cent to 15 per cent, introducing a regressive scale for social taxes with rates ranging from 20 per cent down to 7 per cent, and reducing personal income taxes by lowering the maximum rate from the current 30 per cent to 20 per cent, applicable to all who receive salaries or other income paid in Kazakhstan.

Transfer pricing/tariff policies

In 2001, the government passed transfer pricing legislation, giving tax and customs officials the go-ahead to monitor export-import transactions with a goal to stopping the understating of earnings through export price manipulation. Foreign investors continue to raise concerns that the Organization for Economic Cooperation and Development's (OECD) standards for determining a proper market price under transfer pricing legislation have been ignored. Current practice does not account for all cost and quality differences.

Another disputable issue is the fact that transfer pricing can take place even in transactions between unrelated parties. Across all industry sectors a key factor working against the investment climate is a lack of transparency in setting tariffs. Donors have provided the Kazakhstan Government with significant assistance, but despite their efforts major investors have failed to reach an agreement, meaning the country loses out on investments and much-needed technical resources. The Anti-Monopoly Agency of Kazakhstan needs to adopt reasonable and transparent tariff policies in the nearest future to protect domestic and foreign investors.

Conversion and transfer policies

There are few restrictions on the conversion or transferral of funds associated with an investment into a freely usable currency at a legal market-clearing rate. In 1996, Kazakhstan adopted Article 8 of the International Monetary Fund's (IMF) Articles of Agreement, effectively agreeing that currency conversions and repatriation of investment profits will not be restricted. In 1999 the government and NBK abolished the managed exchange rate system, allowing the national currency (the tenge) to float at market rates.

Bank accounts and foreign currency

Residents and non-residents may open bank accounts with no restrictions. For non-residents, money transfers in currency associated with foreign investments are not restricted. The NBK permits non-residents to pay salaries in cash in foreign currency to both foreign and local employees. Foreign investors may freely convert and repatriate tenge earnings made inside Kazakhstan.

Performance requirements

Performance requirements, excepting domestic content requirements, are negotiated as part of a contract between the investor and the Committee on Investments under the Ministry of Foreign Affairs. Usually an investor's obligations include financial requirements, responsibility for training local specialists and financial or other material contributions to social funds and community or regional infrastructure development (including schools, hospitals and health facilities).

These requirements are often central to investment contracts. It is not unheard of for companies to be required to rebuild factories and plants, provide back pay to workers who may not have been paid for several months and meet imposed production targets. There are cases where contracts have been revoked because performance obligations were not met. The Committee on Investments is responsible for monitoring the fulfillment of these obligations. The government may revoke the operating licence of the company if the committee determines that it has not met its financial or other contractual obligations.

In order to obtain the benefits and privileges of investing in Kazakhstan, an investor must provide the agency with detailed information on technical and financial details of the proposed project. With the exception of investments in oil production and mining, rules on domestic content and financing are not applied universally.

The Customs Code

Kazakhstan adopted international tariff terminology as its basis but as yet it has not been published in full. As a result, customs offices in the regions continue to use the old tariff schedules, causing unnecessary delays in processing and increased costs for importers. Under the new code, major principles of modern customs administration have been introduced, although in general terms that still need to be more fully defined.

WTO accession

Liberal trade policies and legislation to bring trade regimes in line with WTO standards have been in force since before 1996 when Kazakhstan submitted its *Memorandum on the Foreign Trade Regime* leading to the first round of consultations on WTO accession in 1997. By late 2005, Kazakhstan's WTO Accession Working Party had met seven times. Under WTO Trade-Related Aspects of Intellectual Property Rights (TRIPS) obligations Kazakhstan does not comply. No clear protection for pre-existing works or sound recordings under copyright law exists. Kazakhstan has not ratified the '1997 World Intellectual Property Organization Copyright Treaty' or the 'Performances and Phonograms Treaty'. Kazakhstan is on the United State's Trade Representative's (USTR) 'priority watch list' for intellectual property right (IPR) violations. Bilateral negotiations are required to comply with WTO standards. Although Kazakhstan has enacted a number of laws and changed many policies during the last few years, several changes are still required. The speed in which Kazakhstan can proceed on this depends on the government's willingness to make tough decisions.

Privatization

Since 1995, the government has privatized many large-scale companies completely and has sold majority shares in other companies to foreign investors. Privatization advanced rapidly during 1996 and 1997 in all sectors of the economy, including oil and gas, power generation, coal, and telecommunications. In 1998, due to low oil prices, President Nazarbayev announced that the government would suspend future privatizations in the oil and gas sector.

National treatment is denied in the petroleum and subsurface sectors. In June 2002, the then Prime Minister (**Imangali Tasmagambetov**) signed a decree with regulations to implement domestic content requirements, which were originally enacted in 1999 through amendments to the Oil Law and the Subsurface Use Law. The laws require investors to contract

Kazakhstan service providers and to purchase Kazakhstan-produced equipment, goods and raw materials. The 2002 decree required implementation of a designated government body to approve all tender documents, participate in tender committees and approve the decisions of those tender committees in order to ensure compliance with these requirements. The requirements will be challenged in connection with Kazakhstan's WTO accession negotiations since they appear to breach the General Agreement on Tariffs and Trade (GATT) and General Agreement on Trade and Services (GATS) rules as well as the Agreement on Trade Related Investment Measures.

Although foreign investors have the right to participate in all privatization projects, many have concerns regarding the insulation of their potential investments from decrees and legislative changes, most of which do not grandfather existing investments. In addition to arbitrary tax inspections and corruption issues, foreign investors also complain of problems with closure on contracts, delays and irregular practices in licensing.

Dispute settlement

Kazakhstan is still in the process of building its court system, which is often criticized as being unsophisticated and corrupt. Until reform is complete, the performance of courts in the country will be less than optimal for foreign investors to settle their disputes.

Kazakhstan ratified the 'New York Convention on the Recognition and Enforcement of Foreign Arbitral Awards' in 1995 (and other major treaties setting forums for dispute resolution) and adopted the Law on Arbitration Courts and Law on International Commercial Arbitration on 28 December 2004, which permit the local and international commercial arbitral tribunals to adjudicate only those disputes which 'arise from civil contracts'. The above and other treaties take precedence over Kazakhstan's domestic laws and prescribe that all awards rendered by a foreign or international arbitral tribunal would be recognized and enforced in Kazakhstan.

The awards of international commercial arbitration may be enforced through the state enforcement bodies by reference to the relevant national court and may be refused enforcement only on the grounds stated in the International Commercial Arbitration Law. In fact, these grounds fully correlate with such grounds listed in the New York Convention, 1958.

Thus, in accordance with the recently adopted arbitration laws, awards of both international and domestic arbitral tribunals are enforceable in Kazakhstan. The recent amendments to the Code of Civil Procedure set out separate procedures for enforcement of awards of arbitral tribunals and international commercial arbitration. The Ministry of Justice and the Foreign Investors' Council are drafting a law that will mandate the enforcement of arbitral awards. Until this process is complete, arbitration awards are not clearly enforceable within the territory of Kazakhstan.

Right to private ownership and establishment

Foreign and domestic private entities have the right to establish and own business enterprises, and to engage in all forms of remunerative activity. Private entities can buy and sell interests in business enterprises with no restrictions. Under the 2003 Land Code, only Kazakh citizens or companies may own land. The law permits only state-owned entities to use land on a permanent basis. Short-term leases are allowed for a duration of not longer than five years. Long-term leases may be allowed for up to 49 years. Foreigners may rent land for agricultural purposes for up to 10 years or purchase land via a Kazakhstan-registered joint venture (JV) or full subsidiary.

Protection of property rights

Secured interests in property are recognized under the Civil Code and Land Code. Mortgage lending exists but is still in an early stage of development. The NBK created a national mortgage agency to issue bonds secured by mortgages purchased from banks. All property and lease rights for real estate should be registered with special government-owned real estate offices in cities and rural district centres. Kazakhstan's Civil Code protects intellectual property although enforcing IPRs remains difficult. To date there is no adequate legal regime for IPR. Piracy of copyrighted products is widespread and enforcement measures are limited.

Licensing

The 1995 Law on Licensing established the legal framework for licensing activities in Kazakhstan. In 1998, additional procedural acts were adopted to implement the requirements of the law. Within one month of receiving all required documents from a company, the authorized agency must issue the necessary licence. In practice however, this law is inadequate because the government has not yet approved most of the qualifying procedural requirements for the issuing of most licences. This situation creates an unpleasant predicament for some businesses and leaves them vulnerable to inspection bodies that may threaten them with fines or even shut down their activities for failure to procure licences that are often (legally) impossible to obtain.

Capital markets and portfolio investments

Within the CIS, Kazakhstan's laudable efforts to create a sound financial system and a stable macroeconomic framework are unsurpassed. The NBK supervises the banking system and has considerably strengthened it over the past four years. Huge progress in the financial system has begun to allow for financial resource flows to be directed to the most promising sectors of the economy. Official policy supports credit allocation on market terms and the further development of legal, regulatory and accounting systems, which are consistent with international standards and practices. Local banks of the second tier in Kazakhstan have been able to obtain very good ratings from international credit assessment agencies and are now required to meet Basle risk-weighted capital standards.

Margins taken by local banks for credit are high. It is usually more efficient, in terms of both dollars and time, for investors to use retained earnings or borrow from the investor's country of origin. The 10-year-old Kazakhstan Stock Exchange (KASE) is not yet developed to the point of being a source of high-level finance. By February 2006, there were 30 companies with A-listed stock issues, 30 companies with B-listed stock issues and 6 'over-the-counter' issuers (non-listed securities sector). A total of 63 companies have placed corporate bond issues.

Kazakhstan's National Securities Commission has been operating since 1996 in compliance with the norms of the International Organization of Securities Commissioners. In 2001, the commission was placed under the NBK and renamed Securities Market Regulation Department. Kazakhstan has a well-developed infrastructure for equity and debt trading with a network of brokerage firms already established.

In 1998, the government introduced an accumulative pension fund system requiring the mandatory contribution of 10 per cent of the salaries of employed persons. By mid 2005, the 14 accumulation funds in Kazakhstan (13 private and 1 state owned) had US $5 billion in assets, which must be invested in a limited number of instruments including A-listed securities and government bonds.

JSC Law

The new 2003 Law on Joint Stock Companies (JSC Law) provides the basis for regulation of joint stock companies. The JSC Law regulates tender offers for stock of JSCs by requiring the purchaser to notify the Finance Market Regulation Agency and the target company of their intention to purchase 30 per cent or more of the target company and to make an offer to all remaining shareholders to purchase their shares at the price determined by the JSC. There are no laws or regulations specifically authorizing firms to adopt articles of incorporation or association that limit or prohibit foreign investments. The JSC Law allows charter limits on the number of shares or votes that one shareholder may have. The shareholders' general meeting must approve some of corporate actions including mergers and acquisitions.

Double tax treaties and bilateral investment agreements

A total of 40 double taxation treaties plus bilateral investment agreements with more than 30 countries including the United States, United Kingdom, France, Germany, Korea, Russia and Turkey are applicable in Kazakhstan.

Work-permit legislation

Since being introduced nine years ago, work permits and the process for obtaining workplace quotas remain a major concern for investors in Kazakhstan. Implementation is not yet transparent and reflects a negative attitude to foreign workers in the economy. Permits may be tied to conditions that cannot be met within reasonable business operations. The Ministry of Labour has a wide discretion and mandate to implement the work permit process. Procedural delays and other obstacles surrounding the work-permit process can exaggerate this problem.

Regulations for employing foreign labour

On 20 January 2003, Kazakhstan adopted new Rules for Determining the Quota, Conditions and Procedure of Issue of Permits to Employers to Engage Foreign Labour in Kazakhstan as amended (the rules). Compared to earlier legislation, the rules provide a clear, detailed regulation. To obtain a work permit for an employee an employer must apply to the authorized local employment body after completing the established set of procedures; the documents are forwarded to the Ministry of Labour for approval. The following foreign citizens and stateless persons are now exempt from the requirement to obtain a foreign labour work permit:

- directors and GMs of companies with investment projects of the equivalent or greater than US $50 million;
- directors of Kazakhstan companies carrying out investment activities in priority sectors under a contract with an investment authority;
- directors and GMs of banks, insurance and reinsurance institutions;
- representatives of diplomatic missions and international organizations accredited in Kazakhstan;
- representatives of foreign mass media accredited in Kazakhstan;
- representatives of charity and humanitarian organizations registered in Kazakhstan;
- crew of foreign sea and river vessels, aircrafts, railway and motor transport owned by foreign companies;
- actors and athletes working under a contract with a relevant central executive body;
- individual entrepreneurs;
- holders of a residence permit;
- those with refugee status or who have been officially granted political asylum in the Republic of Kazakhstan.

Local labour

Kazakhstan's workforce is highly educated, but the demand for specialized and technically skilled labour (in part due to the extensive development of Kazakhstan's major oil fields) exceeds supply. Experts in management and marketing do not meet demand. Foreign investors employ Kazakhstan's specialists across a wide range of industries, although companies should be prepared to offer additional training (including training abroad) in order to qualify local specialists more fully for their company's needs.

The Labour Law and the Constitution guarantee basic workers' rights. The Law on Professional Labour Unions (1993) provides a legal guarantee against limitations of labour. Kazakhstan joined the International Labour Organization (ILO) in 1993 and has ratified 15 ILO conventions.

Foreign trade zones/free ports

The government established special economic zones in the country's capital, Astana, in July 2001 and on the territory of the Aktau seaport in April 2002. In these special economic zones, foreign and domestic companies are treated equally. Under the law, the Astana Special Economic Zone must be closed by July 2006; the Aktau Special Economic Zone must be closed by January 2007.

The Eurasian Economic Community (EAEC) was established in 2000 as a successor to the unsuccessful Customs Union in order to harmonize customs duties and promote free trade among its partners (including Kazakhstan, Russia, Belarus, Kyrgyzstan and Tajikistan). To date, the EAEC has not been successful in creating a free-trade zone. Kazakhstan permits the importation of goods from EAEC free-trade partners (as well as certain developing or least-developed countries) free of duty or at a reduced rate within the framework of the Generalized System of Preferences.

Positive reasons to invest in Kazakhstan

Kazakhstan is a positive nation to invest in for the following reasons:

- macroeconomic stability;
- huge reserves of natural resources including oil and gas deposits;
- underdeveloped mining of chrome, copper, gold, lead, manganese, silver and uranium;
- EU Most-Favoured-Nation trade agreement;
- few quotas and duties on exports affecting foreign investors;
- no special requirements for engaging in trade-related activities;
- foreign firms may participate in government-financed or -subsidized research and development programmes on a national treatment basis;
- except in banking, media and telecommunications sectors, there are no legal requirements that Kazakh nationals own shares in foreign investments;
- a State Committee for Investments has been established to facilitate foreign investment.

Summary

Kazakhstan has many advantages for investors including an abundance of natural mineral resources, a well-educated workforce and a strong macroeconomic environment, yet it still must compete with alternative destinations for investment dollars. Kazakhstan should not assume that investors in oil and other major industry sectors will continue to accept an unnecessarily onerous investment climate. Certain practices and legislative proposals over a number of years have threatened to take Kazakhstan in the wrong direction at a crucial time in its prosperous development. Much time and effort is spent in dealing with reporting and state agencies. A large sector of the economy is still controlled by national companies. Investors hope that Kazakhstan chooses to continue to move forward, paving the way for future reforms, fair privatization, full integration into the global economy and increased investments.

Key trends in Kazakhstan's energy sector

Sergiy Maslichenko, President of UCELA

Introduction

Kazakhstan's economy is one of the most rapidly growing in the world. Between 2000–2005 the GDP growth averaged some 10 per cent per annum, led by the petroleum sector and supported by a favourable external environment. By 2004, Kazakhstan's oil export revenues constituted 30 per cent of GDP and 60 per cent of all export revenues. The oil sector amounted to 30 per cent of total government revenues.

At the same time, Kazakhstan's transformation into an oil-rich country brings a series of challenges to the economy in general and in particular to the non-oil sector. Natural resources sectors tend to rely on high capital intensity, with low levels of employment and slow technical progress. Economies dominated by those sectors tend to have lower long-term growth, high income and asset inequalities, and face larger volatility associated with changes in commodity prices, such as oil. To avoid negative impact of increasing oil wealth, 'Dutch Disease' phenomena, it is important to develop policies and reforms that support sustainable growth of the non-oil economy.

After a rapid introduction of market reforms in the early years of transition, the momentum of structural reforms has slowed since 2000. A weak judicial system, entrenched vested interests and 'capture' of important sectors combined with a lack of legal and regulatory transparency have resulted in an uneven playing field and a poor investment climate outside the oil and banking sectors, particularly for small- and medium-size domestic and foreign investors.

Confident that demand for their country's oil will expand rapidly, Kazakhstan's leaders are taking an aggressive approach to new exporting and licensing projects. As high oil prices boost Kazakhstan's economic wealth, its government is adopting a tougher negotiating stance with Western investors, while exploring deals with Russian and Chinese companies. Analysts say the government's new approach, which gives the state a higher share of profit from new development projects, is based on a bet that Western conglomerates need Kazakhstan's oil. It is also rooted in Kazakhstan's improving economic climate. With oil priced at US $50 per barrel, Kazakhstan's additional profit power enables it to bargain hard.

For now, foreign investors remain cautious about Kazakhstan's capabilities and prospects. Some observers point out that Kazakhstan continues to grapple with substantial structural risks. In March 2004, the Economist Intelligence Unit research and advisory firm placed a high-risk rating on Kazakhstan's macroeconomic situation. The group's report noted that, 'Kazakhstan suffers from the disadvantage that its oil production costs are relatively high and its tax and legal regimes increasingly unfavourable.' As high oil prices continue to bolster

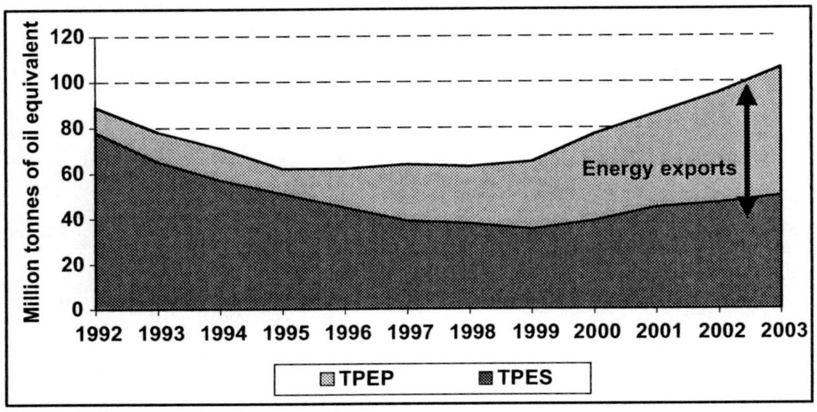

Figure 3.1 Kazakhstan's TPEP and TPES 1992–2003
Source: International Energy Agency.

Kazakhstan's economic health, the country has taken on an aggressive campaign to buy a stake in the international consortium developing the Caspian Sea's Kashagan oil field. The initiative appears to be the latest in a series of steps meant to assert the government's energy interests independently of foreign investors. With a projected 13 billion barrel yield, the Kashagan oil field ranks as the largest oil find in 30 years.

Primary Energy

Kazakhstan is a net energy exporter. Kazakhstan's total primary energy production (TPEP) and total primary energy supply (TPES) are shown in Figure 3.1.

Primary energy production in 2003 in terms of tonnes of oil equivalent (TOE) was approximately 49 per cent oil, 37 per cent coal, 13 per cent gas, and 1 per cent hydro electricity and renewables.

Primary energy consumption is dominated by coal (57.7 per cent), followed by gas (24.0 per cent) and oil (16.7 per cent). Hydropower accounts for 1.5 per cent and renewable sources for only 0.1 per cent (Figure 3.2).

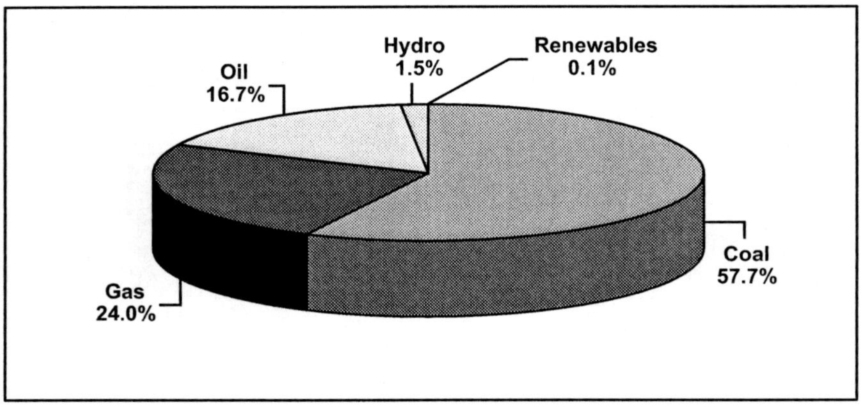

Figure 3.2 Structure of Kazakhstan's TPES in 2003
Source: International Energy Agency.

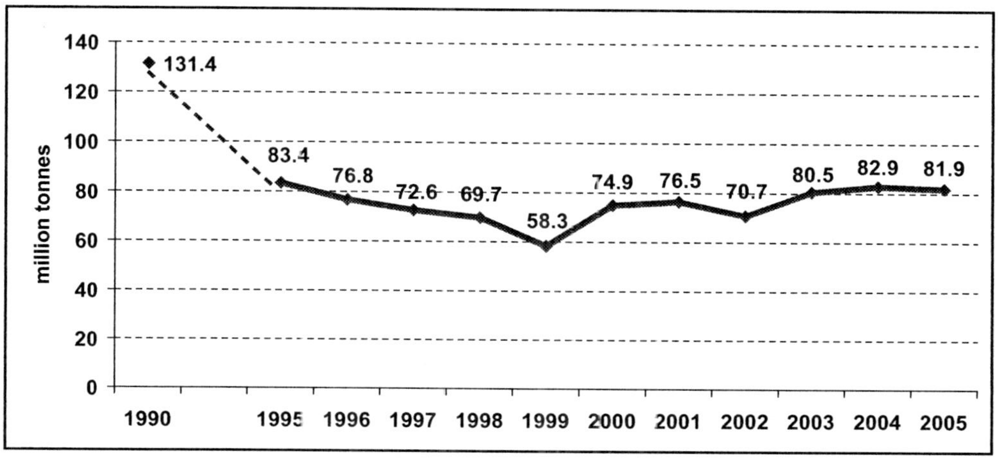

Figure 3.3 Coal production in Kazakhstan 1990–2005
Source: Kazakhstan's Agency for Statistics

Coal

Coal production in Kazakhstan has fallen by 55 per cent since independence. There was, however, a modest upswing in coal production in 2000–2001, but in 2002 the output fell again (Figure 3.3). In 2003–2005 coal production increased by 16%, amounting to 81.9 million tonnes.

Coal production is concentrated in two major deposits at Karaganda and Ekibastuz, which produce 95 per cent of the total. Most of Kazakhstan's coal is extremely high in ash content. Underground mines provide 70 per cent of Kazakhstan's coal and the rest is from open cast mines. (In Karaganda coal is mined primarily by underground methods, while Ekibastuz mines are exclusively open cast.) All coal from Ekibastuz is consigned to electricity generation. Karaganda's coal is used in both the steel and thermal power sectors.

Coal is the primary energy source for electricity generation in Kazakhstan. About 70 per cent of total electricity is generated from coal. The energy sector including the power-generation sector is the main end-user of coal, consuming 65 per cent of total coal supply, followed by industry (16 per cent), households (2 per cent), transport (1 per cent) and agriculture (1 per cent). Net exports have some 15 per cent. Although the coal is inexpensive to produce, there are questions regarding the profitability of exports due to the long distances involved. Markets for Kazakh coal in the former Soviet Union have contracted since 1990, as has the country's internal demand, notwithstanding re-expansion of the economy since 1999.

Oil

Estimates of Kazakhstan's total recoverable oil reserves vary between 95 and 117 billion barrels, with proven reserves between 9 and 29 billion barrels (comparable to the Organisation of the Petroleum Exporting Companies – OPEC – members with Algeria at the low end and Qatar at the high end).

Kazakhstan is the second largest oil producer in the FSU. Between 1999 and 2005 Kazakhstan's oil production (including gas condensate) doubled from 30 million tonnes to 61.9 million tonnes, largely thanks to an inflow of

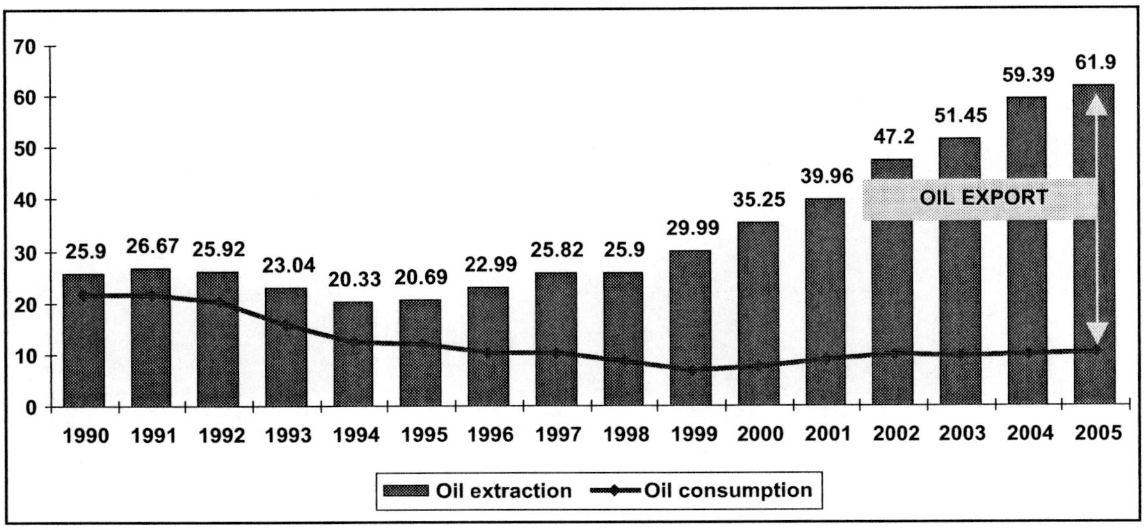

Figure 3.4 Oil extraction including gas condensate, and consumption 1990–2005 (million tonnes)
Source: Kazakhstan's Agency for Statistics

foreign investment (Figure 3.4). Oil exports amounted to 52.4 million tonnes. According to the 'high' and 'low' case scenarios of the government, Kazakhstan oil production is projected to be between 90–120 million tonnes in 2010, and 125–180 million tonnes in 2015.

Kazakhstan has three major oil refineries supplying the northern region (in Pavlodar), western region (in Atyrau) and southern region (in Shymkent), with total refining capacity of about 21 million tonnes per year. In 2003, about 9.5 million tonnes were processed in the refineries, amounting to only 45 per cent of their capacity. Kazakhstan refinery output is characterised by high yields of heavy fuel oil and low yields of high-value light products. This results in large imports of the latter (especially diesel) and exports of the former.

Oil exports

Kazakhstan's oil is exported in three directions: northward (via the Russian pipeline system and rail network); westward (via the Caspian Pipeline Consortium Project and barge to Azerbaijan); and southward (via swaps with Iran). Kazakhstan also exported about 1.5 million tonnes eastward to China by rail in 2005.

The opening of the Caspian Pipeline Consortium (CPC) in 2001, from Western Kazakhstan's Tengiz oilfield to the Black Sea, substantially raised export capacity. Initial capacity of the CPC pipeline is 28 million tonnes per annum, with plans to increase capacity to 67 million tonnes. In 2004, CPC transited roughly 23 million tonnes or 45 per cent of Kazakhstan's exports.

The 1860-mile-long pipeline from North-Western Kazakhstan to China's border is being constructed, which would enable the export of 20 million tonnes per year of Caspian oil to serve China's growing energy needs. Other export routes reportedly under consideration are a possible line to Iran, and a subsea trans-caspian pipeline connecting to the Baku-Tbilisi-Ceyhan project. Oil available for export could reach 50 million tonnes by 2005, 75–100 million tonnes by 2010 and 100–150 million tonnes by 2015.

Natural gas

Estimates of natural gas reserves are around 3 trillion cubic metres, of which 1.8 trillion are considered proven (comparable to Canada and Kuwait). Nearly all of this is associated gas. For some time Kazakhstan gas production has been hampered by lack of infrastructure, leading oil producers to flare gas instead of using it. However, domestic natural gas production tripled from 6.5 billion cubic metres in 1996 to 21.8 billion cubic metres in 2004. The Kazakhstan Government forecasts natural gas gross production will reach 61.4 billion cubic metres by 2010 and 106.1 billion cubic metres by 2015. However, much of this gas is planned to be re-injected into the ground, basically to facilitate oil extraction by maintaining wellhead pressure.

Due to pipeline configurations, Kazakhstan exports much of its own gas production to Russia. At the same time, several regions depend on imported gas. Most imported gas goes to the southern network, which remains almost completely independent on imports via Uzbekistan.

Electricity

The production and consumption of electricity in Kazakhstan fell significantly following independence. Power consumption halved over the period 1990–1999 from 104.7 to 50.7 terawatt hours. However, robust economic growth since 2000 has helped to boost production to 66.8 terawatt hours in 2004 (representing a 33 per cent increase over five years). As a result, since 2002 Kazakhstan has become a net exporter of electricity. Transmission issues, however, force Kazakhstan to import electricity to the southern part of the country, as the country's northern generating units are connected to a separate transmission grid.

Currently Kazakhstan has an overall installed generating capacity of 18,331 megawatts, 87.7 per cent of which is thermal and 12.3 per cent of which is hydroelectric. Thermal-electric power plants (TPP) account for about half of total installed capacity (48.9 per cent), combined heat and power plants (CHP) for 36.6 per cent. Only 2.3 per cent is represented by combined cycle gas turbines (CCGT).

As mentioned above, 70 per cent of the electricity generated in Kazakhstan is produced from coal, followed by hydro (14.6 per cent), gas (10.6 per cent) and oil (4.9 per cent). Industry is the largest consumer of electricity, amounting to 68.7 per cent of total electricity consumption, households account for 9.3 per cent, services for 8 per cent, transport for 5.6 per cent, agriculture for 1.2 per cent and losses for 12.5 per cent (Kazakhstan incurs large energy losses during transmission and distribution over its 25,000 kilometres of power lines, much of which is in need of renewal).

Investment policies

Kazakhstan has been very successful at attracting FDI to its economy. However, in recent years the investment climate has somewhat deteriorated. Private foreign investors do not feel secure enough to make major investments in the country, as the legal 'rules of the game' appear unstable. Given the importance of FDI, the confrontation between the state and the multinationals may result in reducing FDI inflows in the future.

In general, the legal framework developed in the 1990s was designed to attract foreign investors and, therefore, guaranteed stability and protection against adverse changes in the law for a 10-year period following investment or until the expiry of the contract (the Law on Foreign Investment). These guarantees were significantly weakened when the new Tax Code entered into force in 2002. Among other provisions, it was indicated that the taxation conditions could be changed in order to restore the original economic interests of Kazakhstan.

Since 2004 the Kazakhstan government has introduced a new, quite large (up to 33 per cent of adjusted revenues) rent for oil exports. Moreover, the government obliged the national oil and gas company KazMunaiGaz (KMG) to take no less than 50 per cent ownership in each oil project.

However, in May 2004, 47 energy companies sent the government a letter objecting to potential laws that would give the state favourable terms on subsurface exploration. The Kazakhstan Petroleum Association, a lobbying bloc representing multinational corporations, effectively warned the government not to treat itself as a sole provider of regional oil.

Another factor which averts potential investors is corruption. According to the rating issued by Transparency International in 2005, Kazakhstan ranked 107 among 158 countries included in the list (World Business Environment Survey, WB, 2002).

Energy sector legal analysis – the limits of stabilization rights under subsoil use contracts and the effect of destabilizing clauses with respect to mandatory payments

Abai Shaikenov and Yuliya Mitrofanskaya, Salans, Almaty

Introduction

Most investors are concerned about legislative clarity and the ability to work within a stable legal sphere. This is particularly true of ventures that tie up the investor's return for 10 or more years, including subsoil use contracts for petroleum and other mining operations. Unfortunately, Kazakhstan law does not provide precise answers to many questions relating to the stabilization of applicable law and contract stabilization clauses. This gives rise to many disputes between subsoil users and state authorities concerning the effect of later legislative amendments (including, for example, changes to the laws that govern licensing, labor, and ecological safety). This article considers questions that often arise in practice for energy producers: Do stabilization rights really work? Can they be applied when the customs fee rates change? These questions will be considered in relation to the following example.

Example

A subsoil use contract concluded in 1998 (the contract) states that the fees for the customs clearance of crude oil must be paid in accordance with current legislation. Up to July 2003, the subsoil user paid custom fees at rates established by Government Decree No 1479, dated 7 November 1995. These rates varied from 0.2 to 0.4 per cent of the customs value of goods, depending on the customs clearance method. On 10 June 2003, the government adopted a new law under Decree No 669, which changed the fee calculation mechanism (Decree 669).

Under the current law, customs fees must be paid on a fixed rate of 50 euros per main page of cargo customs declaration. The subsoil user complied with the new law and paid custom fees in accordance with Decree 669. However, the customs authorities demanded that the payments should be made in accordance with previous rates, which are based upon customs value of goods. The reasoning for their demand is based on the contract's tax stability regime.

Analysis

In this situation, we believe that the legal stability principle does not apply and the customs authorities' reasoning is specious. We believe that this scenario should be considered under the rubric of the following questions:

- What is legislative stability and contract stability?
- Is it possible to stabilize the amount of customs fees with reference to a date that precedes the customs clearance of goods?
- Does the amount of customs fee constitute a contractual condition?
- How does the application of new laws on customs fees depend on the increase or decrease of customs fees?
- What is legislative stability and contract stability?

Under Kazakhstan law there is no broad principle of legislative stability. The Constitution (Article 77.3), Criminal Code (Article 5) and Law on Normative Legal Acts (24 March 2004, Article 37) all contain clauses that outlaw the retroactive application of legislation where it imposes new responsibilities or obligations on citizens. However, in cases where a new law softens or abolishes these responsibilities or obligations then it will be retroactive. Similar clauses are also set out in the Code on Administrative Violations (Article 6). These apply not only to citizens, but also to legal entities. In the Civil Code, legislative stability is defined as 'the lack of retroactive application of civil legal acts and applicability of new laws to civil relations that arise from new laws' (Article 4).

With respect to contracts, the stability principle is characterized a bit differently. Contractual conditions remain in force when the applicable law changes, except in cases when the law expressly requires its application to relations that arise from existing agreements (Civil Code, Article 383). Laws on subsoil and subsoil use and on petroleum have similar clauses on stability. These provide that 'amendments and changes to legislation that worsen the subsoil user's (contractor's) conditions shall not apply to activities under contracts concluded prior to the introduction of such amendments and changes'.

Under the Law on Investment, the Republic of Kazakhstan guarantees the stability of contracts concluded between investors and state authorities, except where amendments are made by the agreement of the parties (Law On investments, 8 January 2003, Article 4). Exceptions to this rule include amendments to laws that regulate excise goods, national and ecological safety, healthcare and morality. In these cases, an amendment to the contract is necessary (Law On investments, 8 January 2003, Article 4; Republic of Kazakhstan Law on Subsoil and Subsoil Use, Article 71). The subsoil contract tax matters are separately stabilized. In these cases, the tax regime is stabilized until the end of the contract term. The only exception to this rule is where the contracting parties amend their agreement in order to maintain the 'balance of economic interests' of the parties (Law on Taxes, Article 94-3; Tax Code, Article 285).

Accordingly, under current laws there are no universal stability rules. As a general observation, prevailing laws govern social relationships as and when they arise. The law provides for certain exceptions to this rule, allowing the regulation of 'earlier' civil law relationships by 'new' retroactive legislation or by 'old' stabilized legislation. In the latter event, the parties must solemnize this arrangement by contract. For example, the Tax Law stabilizes the terms and rates of taxation for subsoil users (Tax Code, Article 282.2; Republic of Kazakhstan Law on Taxes, Article 94). If a law is not stabilized, then newly created relationships falling under that law will be governed by current legislation.

These exceptional cases notwithstanding, the general rule is that the laws applicable to a contract are not to change. For subsoil use contracts, laws that worsen a subsoil user's position are not applicable to activities under those contracts. Taxation is similarly stabilized.

Is it possible to stabilize the amount of customs fees with reference to a date preceding the customs clearance of goods?

Under the Law on Taxes which was in effect as of the date of the contract:

> *A tax regime established under subsoil use contracts... operates without changes until the end of the contract term, except for the cases when changes to the contract's tax regime are introduced by the agreement of the parties to the contract and do not result in a change to the primary economic interest ratio of Republic of Kazakhstan and subsoil users on contracts (Law on Taxes, Article 94-3).*

The tax regime includes contractual tax provisions and tax laws in force as at the contract's effective date. However, until the Tax Code came into force, customs fees and payments did not fall come under the definition of the term 'tax regime'. The Law on Taxes provided that:

> *Tax legislation of the Republic of Kazakhstan consists of this Law, which establishes mandatory payments of a tax nature... and regulates taxation relationships in the Republic of Kazakhstan (except for issues of customs fees that are regulated by special legislation...) (Law on Taxes, Article 1).*

Accordingly, the Law on Taxes directly excluded customs fees from the ambit of tax legislation. In addition, those Articles of the Law on Taxes, which set out the full list of national and municipal taxes and fees, did not reference 'customs fees' (Law on Taxes, Articles 3 and 4). Customs fees were first included in the list of other mandatory payments to the budget when the Tax Code of the Republic of Kazakhstan (dated 12 June 2001) was adopted (Article 59 and 64). It follows that the tax laws (including Article 94-3 of the Law on Taxes) granting tax regime stability do not apply to the regulation of customs fee payments. This means that the calculation and payment of customs fees for the custom clearance of goods does not fall under a stabilized tax regime. Therefore, any assertion that customs fees are fixed under the stabilized tax regime of a subsoil use contract is not supported by law.

The Law on Customs in force at the Contract's effective date stated that:

> *Except for the cases established... by legal acts of the Republic of Kazakhstan in force at the moment of accepting customs declarations and documents that are necessary for custom purposes, shall apply to the Custom Activities (Law on Customs, Article 6).*

The current Customs Code contains similar conditions (Customs Code, Article 5). Accordingly, the amounts of customs fees for custom clearance are not and were not subject to stabilization.

The Law on Customs stipulated only one situation when customs fee could be decided by contract. The exception relates to the importation of goods by subsoil users under an investment contract (See Law on Customs, clause 7, Article 149 and Republic of Kazakhstan Law On Foreign Investments, 27 December 1994, Article 22). The current Customs Code similarly sanctions the stabilization of certain customs rules only for customs fee exemptions and tariff preferences. The Customs Code also reads that:

> ***Privileges provided on the basis of contracts, which are concluded prior to the date of effect of this code, in accordance with the Republic of Kazakhstan Law On Custom activities, under the condition of their non-application, remain in force until the date stipulated in those contracts (Customs Code, Article 531.2).***

The foregoing situations are not applicable to our hypothetical case, because they relate to customs privileges, which were not available to subsoil users at the time of the contract.

In summary, the laws in force at the moment of export-import operation govern the payment of custom fees. Aside from privileges under investment contracts, neither the Law on Customs nor the Customs Code provides for exceptions from this rule. Therefore, there would appear to be no legal basis for stabilizing the customs rates to the effective date of a subsoil use contract.

Does the amount of a customs fee constitute a contractual condition?

Under the law, an agreement is defined as an arrangement between two or more persons concerning the establishment, amendment or cessation of civil rights and obligations (Civil Code of the Republic of Kazakhstan, Article 378.1). An agreement is concluded if the parties agree on all material terms of the contract (Civil Code of the Republic of Kazakhstan, Article 393.1). Under the contract stabilization principle, the conditions of a contract remain in force even after the amendment of applicable civil legislation. The only exception arises when the new law specifically states its retroactive application. Therefore, the above question is of capital importance.

In order to answer this question, it is necessary to understand that the civil law applies only to civil law relationships. According to the Civil Code:

> ***Civil legislation shall not apply to property relations which are based on the administrative or any other power subordination of one party by the other, including tax and other budget relations, except for the cases provided for by legislative acts (Civil Code of the Republic of Kazakhstan, Article 1).***

Accordingly, civil law rules that stipulate the priority of a contract and other conditions are applicable only to the contract's civil law conditions. In other words, the civil law can only establish priority rights where the matter concerned falls under its jurisdiction, and not under some other field of legislation.

Customs fees are 'obligatory payments to the budget' and rules governing the payment of the same are based on the administrative power of the state. In these cases, an exporter or importer of goods is subject to the administrative jurisdiction of state authorities who supervise customs dealings in accordance with the law. The payment of customs fees falls under public law and is not a civil law contract. This means that the amount and payment of customs fees cannot be a contractual condition. This is an imperative provision of law. Accordingly, any stability protections afforded under civil legislation do not apply to the consideration of customs payments. Even if a contract purports to set out customs payment rates, such provisions do not constitute contractual conditions.

In our example, the contract states that the payment of custom fees must be made in the amount determined by legislation. Aside from the question of privileges, the customs law did not permit the fixing of custom fees by subsoil use contract. Therefore, the prevailing customs rules (whether included in the contract or not) apply and are paramount to any contractual terms purported to speak to the matter. This means that it is not possible to definitively assert that a subsoil user should pay fees on rates stated by contract. These rates must be in the amount prescribed by law.

Similar provisions in the current legislation support this view. The Tax Code states that the government establishes custom fee rates (Tax Code, Article 515). Furthermore, the Customs Code stipulates that 'customs fee rates are established by the government and come into force after 30 calendar days of their official publication' (Customs Code, Article 292.2). This means that any changes to the administrative law will affect a contract falling under its sphere, irrespective of whether the contract provides otherwise.

How does the application of new laws on customs fees depend on the increase or decrease of customs fees?

Notwithstanding the foregoing, the answer to the above question will be different depending on whether custom fees are increased or decreased.

Subsoil use and investment legislation protects subsoil-users and investors from the application of new laws that worsen their position under their contracts. In the case of an increase of customs fees, the subsoil user would continue making payments in the amounts established under the old legislation. But what happens if the new law decreases the customs fees?

Under the Law On Foreign Investments (which applies to contracts concluded prior to 2003), the parties could change the contract with an aim of achieving a balance of interests (Law On Foreign Investments, 27 December 1994, Article 6). The tax legislation has similar provisions on the 'correction' of taxation terms under subsoil use contracts, in order to maintain the balance of economic interests (Law on Taxes, Article 94-3 and Tax Code, Article 285). Therefore, many subsoil use contracts were changed after the decrease of the tax rates. However, there are strong arguments that a decrease of customs fees automatically applies to the subsoil use contracts without the need to amend the same (at least those contracts concluded before the enactment of the Tax Code).

First, customs fees do not form part of a stabilized contractual tax regime. Second, the terms governing the payment of customs fees are not contractual conditions. As such, their inclusion into the contract does not mean that parties have agreed to the payment of customs fees in such amounts. Finally, customs legislation always stipulates that customs fees should be paid on prevailing rates.

Conclusion

Not all of the provisions in a subsoil use contract are contractual conditions enjoying stability. In order to determine whether a particular condition in a contract is stabilized, one must examine whether that condition falls under civil law or administrative law.

Customs legislation applying to subsoil use contracts concluded prior to the enactment of the Tax Code does not stabilize customs fee rates. Nor does this legislation require the amendment of the contract in order to maintain economic interests of the parties. As a general rule, customs fees are paid at rates established by prevailing legislation. When custom fees are decreased, the subsoil user pays the decreased amounts. When custom fees are increased, the subsoil user pays the old, lower amount, because it is stabilized against legislative changes that worsen its position.

Recent legal developments in Kazakhstan's business legislation – an overview of changes in the legal framework since 2003

Salans, Almaty

Introduction

By any measure, the Republic of Kazakhstan has considerable development potential. The country sits upon some of the largest petroleum and natural gas fields in the world, among them Karachaganak, Tengiz and Uzen. The country also holds enormous reserves of gold, diamonds, chromium, coal and other valuable minerals across its vast territory.

What is less well known is that Kazakhstan also has a very stable government and political system and a well-educated, well-trained workforce, as well as highly developed industrial and agricultural sectors that offer significant export possibilities. In addition, the country has good transportation infrastructure, especially in regards to its highways and railroads, which link the great distances separating the country's products from its markets.

After a rather slow start during the years immediately following independence, Kazakhstan is rapidly putting into place the legal elements necessary to attract foreign investors to assist in the creation of a dynamic market economy. In fact, to a degree greater than most of the newly independent states of the former Soviet Union, the Republic of Kazakhstan has enacted an impressive body of commercial and fiscal legislation to govern investment activity. The establishment of a stable legislative framework to govern foreign investment is important for winning the confidence of the foreign investment community eager to tap into the enormous natural resources wealth of the country.

The past two years in particular have resulted in certain amendments to legislation in the Republic of Kazakhstan. These have had a major impact, sometimes less attractively, on the foreign investment climate.

Corporate Law – changes to Kazakhstan's Law on Joint Stock Companies and Law on Partnerships with Limited and Additional Liability.

Joint-Stock Companies

On 13 May 2003, a new law on Joint-Stock Companies (JSC Law) was adopted. Several amendments have already been introduced into the JSC

Law since the date of its adoption; however the most substantial changes to JSC Law have been made by the Amending Law dated 8 July 2005 (Amending Law). The following summarizes some of the notable changes of the Amending Law.

Amended definition of voting shares

The definition of voting shares was changed to provide that shares of shareholders of record 'about which there is no data available in the record system of the central securities depository' shall not have voting rights (the impact of this provision on shares held by nominees is uncertain).

Elimination of People's Joint-Stock Company concept

According to the Amending Law the defining term and the articles and provisions regulating People's Joint-Stock Companies (ie larger JSCs with their own capital of not less than 1 million times the monthly calculated indices and a certain number of shareholders, not less than 500) were totally excluded from the JSC Law.

Charter capital

Pursuant to the Amending Law the charter capital must be denominated in national currency (tenge). In contrast to the former edition, the amended JSC Law specifies that an increase of the charter capital is carried out through allocation of the declared shares of the company. Such increase is now not done upon the court decision or decision of the general meeting of shareholders. Since a decision on allocation of the shares of the company within the quantity of the declared shares is made by the Board of Directors, the increase of the charter capital may be carried out upon the decision of this body.

Requirements to the charter provisions

One of the noteworthy changes is the provision that mandates disclosure in the charter by the shareholders and responsible individuals of the JSC of their affiliated entities. In addition to the charter, the Amending Law introduced one more document, the Corporate Governance Code of the JSC, which regulates relations in the process of management, such as relations between the shareholders and other bodies of the company and between these bodies and interested persons. However, adoption of the code is not a mandatory requirement and can be introduced by the company at its own discretion and if such an option is permitted under the charter of the company. The code must also be approved by the general meeting of shareholders.

Changes in the exclusive authorities of the General Meeting of Shareholders

Among others, the General Meeting of Shareholders now has the power to approve and amend the Code of Corporate Management of the JSC (the in-house law that regulates the relationship of shareholders and the JSC). The General Meeting of Shareholders also is empowered to increase declared shares and to change the kind of declared yet-to-be-issued shares of the JSC. On the other hand, the requirement that the General Meeting of Shareholders of a JSC approves 'an increase of the liabilities of the company by an amount constituting twenty five per cent or more of the amount of the capital of JSC' was eliminated – now it is only required to have the Board of Directors' approval (which was already required for such increases of 10 per cent or more unless otherwise required by a particular company's charter).

Also, approval of the decision on conclusion by the company of the major transactions and transactions, in which the company is interested, is now excluded from the exclusive competence of the General Meeting of Shareholders. Now the decision of the Board of Directors would suffice for the execution of a major transaction. As for the execution of the transaction in which the company is interested, the decision of the Board of Directors is also required, except for in certain instances as set forth below; however, such decision must be taken by a simple majority of the votes of members of the Board of Directors, who may not be interested in striking such a transaction.

Changes in the exclusive authorities of the Board of Directors

A substantial movement away from the exclusive competence of the Board of Directors is the approval procedure regarding the expenditure of reserve capital funds. As noted above, the Board of Directors' authority has been extended in regards to the execution of major transactions and transactions in which the company is interested.

Membership in the Board of Directors

According to Article 54, no less than one-third of the members of the JSC's Board of Directors must be independent directors who are unaffiliated with the company (unless the person is the independent director of this company), its affiliated persons or entities. Additionally, they must have no subordination relationship with the management of the company or its affiliated entities and must not be an auditor of the company at present or have been for the previous three years, unless otherwise provided for by the law.

Definition of a major transaction

The definition of a major transaction was amended and now applies to transactions for the purchase or alienation (or 'which may result in the company's purchase or alienation') of assets having a value equal to 25 percent of the total value of the company's assets. Therefore, a broader range of transactions (eg the pledge of property in connection with a loan) will now be considered as a major transaction. As mentioned above, it is no longer a requirement that the General Meeting of Shareholders approve major transactions, although the charter of a company may set out a list of major transactions requiring shareholder approval.

Changes in regard to transactions in which the company is interested

The following transactions are not classified as transactions in which the company is interested: 1) transaction on undertaking the obligations on confidentiality with respect to the information containing banking, commercial or other secrets protected by the law; 2) the transaction of the company with its affiliated entity or person, which has been executed in accordance with the legislation of the Republic of Kazakhstan on state procurement.

As mentioned above, the Board of Directors makes the decision whether they will or won't enter into such transaction. However, the General Meeting of Shareholders does make a decision on such a transaction (by voting) in the case where all members of the Board of Director are interested persons or when the decision can't be made by the Board of Directors due to an absence of the qualified number of votes required. The JSC Law now also provides the option to define an alternative procedure for the conclusion of certain types of transactions in which the company is interested.

JSC affiliated entities

Article 64 of the Amending Law provides that the affiliated entity can be an individual, a relative or the spouse of a principal shareholder or of any JSC official. The JSC is obligated to keep all affiliated entities on records.

Extension of the period for amending a JSC's foundation documents

The period for amending a JSC's foundation documents (ie charter) and to bring the amount of charter capital in line with the requirement of the new JSC Law (50,000 times the monthly calculated indices), in order to comply with the law adopted in 2003, was two years and expired in May 2005; this period has now been extended for another year until May 2006.

Limited liability partnership

Substantial amendments to the Law on Partnerships with Limited and Additional Liability (the LLP Law), 22 April 1998, were introduced in May 2003. One of the reasons behind these amendments was the adoption of the Law on Joint Stock Companies, 13 May 2003 (the JSC Law).

The JSC Law dictated a substantial increase of the minimum amount of the JSC's charter capital. Small-sized JSCs ended up reorganizing into LLPs since they failed to satisfy the requirement of the new JSC Law. The LLP Law was amended in this regard to accommodate for procedures needed for the reorganization of a JSC into an LLP. The amendments to this effect included the following:

- A JSC that reorganizes into an LLP and that consists of more than 100 shareholders is not required to have a foundation agreement.
- A JSC that reorganizes into an LLP and that consists of more than 100 shareholders would be provided by the registering authority with the list of documents required to effect reorganization.
- An entry must be made into the register of the LLP participants shortly after the new participant has joined the LLP, where such LLP was reorganized from a JSC that consisted of more than 100 shareholders.
- LLPs consisting of more than 100 participants have the right to keep the register of participants. Such a register must be kept by a licensed professional of the securities market. The LLP would conclude an agreement with such professional. For example, title to the shares in the capital of LLP (that was reorganized from the JSC) with number of participants exceeding 100 is certified by the extract from such register.

Other amendments to the LLP Law were introduced with a view to removing contradictions of the law with other special and general legal acts of the Republic of Kazakhstan (such as the Land Law, rules on registration of reorganized entities, etc).

Currency control and banking

A new law on currency regulation and currency control (the Currency Law) was adopted on 13 June 2005 and came into force on 18 December 2005. Additionally, the NBK , as the agency responsible for currency control regulation, adopted new legal acts for the implementation of the Currency Law – Rules 134 (Rules for Carrying out Currency Transactions in Republic of Kazakhstan approved by the Resolution of the NBK Board No 134, 29 October 2005) and Rules 122 (Rules for Carrying Out of Monitoring Over Currency Operations of Non-Residents that Perform Activity in the Republic of Kazakhstan approved by the Resolution of the NBK Board No 122 14 October 2005) – and amended the previous NBK Instruction on Organisation of Export and Import Currency Control in the Republic of Kazakhstan.

General observations

The new Currency Law brought about a number of changes with regard to currency control. The major novelty of the Currency Law was that it provided for a softening and/or an abolishment of the licensing regime from 1 January 2007 and a switch to the registration and notification regime of currency operations. Thus, currently there are three levels of currency control: notification regime, registration regime and licensing regime.

Notification regime

The notification regime is the least burdensome procedure, requiring that the NBK be notified of the currency operation and that the NBK issue confirmation of the receipt of such notification. The notification duty is imposed on:

- banks when, under their 'own' operations, the debt to a non-resident exceeds US $300,000 or the debt of a non-resident exceeds US $10,000;
- other residents and professional participants of the securities market acquiring securities or shares of investment funds contributing to charter capitals or conducting operations related to derivatives;
- individuals opening accounts with foreign banks located in OECD-member countries or international members of the Financial Action Task Force (FATF) on money laundering;
- legal entities (excluding banks) opening accounts at foreign banks;
- any residents/non-residents acquiring ownership rights to immovable property.

Registration Regime

Registration requirements arise in cases when/of:

- debt to a non-resident exceeds US $300,000 or the debt of the non-resident exceeds US $10,000;
- commercial credits are extended or financial loans are advanced for more than 180 days or, if extended or advanced for less than 180 days, the credit/loan is factually repaid after 180 days;
- direct investments;
- acquisition of intellectual property rights;
- performance by residents of obligations of a participant of joint activity;
- a resident legal entity opens accounts with foreign banks designated for financing expenses connected to maintenance of branches and representative offices of this legal entity.

However, a number of operations are exempted from registration, eg banks' 'own' operations; agreements on sovereign foreign loans or sovereign guarantee loans; acquisition by non-residents of state securities issued in Kazakhstan; acquisition of Kazakhstan depository receipts by non-residents; and currency operations carried out by Kazakhstan state establishments located abroad.

Licensing regime

Obtaining a licence is required when:

- a resident grants 'commercial credit' to a non-resident in an amount exceeding US $10,000 for a period exceeding 180 days (or 365 days with respect to certain goods as specified in the list established by the government);
- for certain operations related to participation in the charter capital, operations with securities and derivative instruments;
- a resident opens a bank account in foreign banks (with a number of exceptions).

Banking legislation

In late December 2005, an amendment law (the Amendment Law) was passed introducing a number of amendments to over 10 legal acts affecting the regulation and supervision of financial services in Kazakhstan. Below the most notable changes are described.

Removal of limitations on banks with foreign participation

The Amendment Law abolished a number of restrictions relating to Kazakhstan banks with foreign participation. Importantly, the law abolished the limitation on the ratio of foreign equity to the aggregate equity in a Kazakhstan bank. Additionally, other requirements specifying required proportions of Kazakhstan citizens in the management and wider staff of banks were abolished as well.

Abolishment of a licensing requirement with respect to commercial lending

Another important development introduced by the Amendment Law was the abolishment of the long debated licensing requirement with respect to commercial lending activity. The Amendment Law substituted the term 'lending operations' with the term 'banking lending operations' as a result of which now only banks, mortgage-companies, brokers/dealers with rights as nominal holders and wholly owned state subsidiary companies need a licence in order to engage in commercial lending activities.

Importantly, the above substitution of terms was also made in tax legislation causing uncertainty with respect to the application of VAT on commercial lending services rendered by unlicensed persons. Under Kazakhstan's Tax Code, only licensed financial services are exempt from VAT. Given the introduction of the term 'banking lending operations' it would appear that lending operations carried out by entities, which are not banks, mortgage companies, brokers/dealers having rights as nominal holders or 100 per cent state subsidiary companies, are now subject to VAT. The major issue that has arisen in effect of this amendment relates to the VAT calculation method *vis-à-vis* lending services. Due to the lack of any satisfactory practice on this issue, it is yet to be clarified by Kazakhstan's tax authorities.

Mineral Resource Development Law

On 1 December 2004 Kazakhstan's President Nursultan Nazarbayev signed Law No 2-III on Introduction of Amendments and Additions into Certain Legal Acts on Subsoil Use and Subsoil Operations (the Subsoil Amending Law), which became effective as of 8 December 2004. The Subsoil Amending Law has introduced changes to the former Presidential Edict (now a law) No 2828 On Subsoil and Subsoil Use (27 January 1996) as amended (the Subsoil Law) and the former Presidential Edict (now a law) No 2350 On Petroleum (28 June 1995) as amended (the Petroleum Law), both being the legislative cornerstones for petroleum industry in the Republic of Kazakhstan. Below, the focus will be on notable changes to the legal regime of subsoil use operations post the previous 1999 substantial amendments.

Types of subsoil use contracts

Prior classification as 'exploration', 'production' and 'combined exploration and production' contracts was replaced with three new forms of contracts in the wake of surrendering the licence-based regime. The Subsoil Amending Law introduced: 1) production sharing agreements; 2) concession agreements; and 3) service agreements and provides for 'combined and other forms of contracts' depending on the conditions of specific operations and other circumstances.

Under Subsoil Use Law (Article 42) and Petroleum Law (Article 25), which both contain identical provisions, 'Conclusion, performance and termination of a contract shall be carried out in accordance with this [Subsoil Use] law and the civil legislation of the Republic of Kazakhstan'. However, the provisions of the Subsoil Law take precedence over civil law where the matter is not provided for under the general provisions of civil law (Article 4(3) of Subsoil Law and Articles 1(3) and 1(4) of Kazakhstan Civil Code).

Tender rules, role of national company, strategic partner

As before, the subsurface use rights (meaning 'exploration', 'production' and 'combined exploration and production') may be acquired from the government's competent Ministry of Energy and Mineral Resources (MEMR) via two methods: tender or direct negotiations. Please note that the tenderer may partake with the National Company without tender as the 'strategic partner' (see below) or where a special tender is organized that predetermines a mandatory share of KMG.

KMG now has the right of mandatory share (not less than 50 per cent) in any block selected for tender upon the discretion of the MEMR and may acquire the property of interest without tender where the latter elects a 'direct negotiations' method for that purpose. The new Production Sharing for Petroleum Operations On the Sea Law (PSA Law), 23 July 2005, also sets this provision with regard to offshore blocks developed under the PSA regime.

As defined in the Petroleum Law, a 'strategic partner' is a Kazakh or foreign entity (or consortium thereof) chosen by the National Company upon consultation with the competent authority (meaning the MEMR). This is based on the criteria of the Subsoil Use Law for the implementation of a project by direct negotiations between the National Company and the competent authority, or in accordance with a treaty ratified by the Republic of Kazakhstan. It appears that the Kazakhstan Government made the salient exception from the general tendering rule to minimize KMG's share of exploration risks on large-sized blocks (which expenditures are always high given the uncertainty of geological work). Further, the 'strategic partner' would be obligated, under Petroleum Law Article 7–1, to pay the signing bonus and carry KMG during the exploration phase unless the joint operating agreement establishes otherwise.

State pre-emptive right

One of the most important changes that the Subsoil Amending Law has introduced is the state's pre-emptive right to buy out a share in any subsoil use projects (as the law generally defines mineral resources) whenever the current operator announces its intention to sell the share. What is specifically 'guaranteed' to a potential seller is that this provision has the retroactive effect to all existing subsoil use contracts (the Subsoil Use Law Article 71 states expressly so) irrespective of the 'grandfathering' clause that normally any E&P contract has incorporated.

Finally, the cited article expressly provides for the reach of the state's pre-emptive right not only to its interest directly in the project or the entity that holds the contractual rights but also to the entity that may, directly or indirectly, make decisions or influence the decision-making process of the seller (if the principal activities of such entity are connected with subsoil use operations in Kazakhstan). Similarly, Article 53 of the Petroleum Law repeats this requirement in the context of the general transfer permission rule.

Pledge of subsoil rights

In addition to the MEMR consent requirement, banks are now on equal legal footing with any other pledgor. Another noteworthy change is the general permission to refer pledgee/pledgor relationship to the provisions of Civil Code.

Local content

Aimed at protecting the domestic market, the Subsoil Amending Law has, once again, repeated the preference requirement with respect to Kazakhstan goods and services, conditional to the satisfaction of state and/or international standards, and has introduced a 20 per cent discount to local bidders in this regard (Article 63-2/3) of the Subsoil Use Law).

Some of the new obligations of the 'subsoil user'

In dealings with tenders, the Subsoil Law and the new PSA Law now retain the focus on tenderer's proposals to develop high technologies, new processing and refining facilities, trunk and other pipelines, construction and joint use of infrastructure and other facilities.

MEMR now has the right to mandate amounts of crude oil to be supplied to domestic refineries based on the country's needs, project feasibility studies, contracts, price and other factors (Article 6.1 of the Petroleum Law).

Another new obligation to the parties of subsoil use contracts is an agreement on the level of salary payable to Kazakhstan staff hired to carry out work under the contract, which is subject to annual indexation under the official refinancing rate of Kazakhstan's National Bank (Article 42/2/2–4) of the Subsoil Law).

Gas Flaring/Utilization

Generally speaking, flaring of associated and/or natural (free) gas is now prohibited except in the cases of emergency situations and/or threat to health or the environment (Article 30–5 of the Petroleum Law). The general prohibition provision will not apply to contractors that had their gas utilization programme approved before 1 December 2004 until such programme has ended, or to contractors without an approved gas utilization programme if such a programme will be developed and approved by the responsible state agency prior to 1 July 2006.

Dispute resolution

Under the Subsoil Law (Article 71–2) and the Petroleum Law (Article 58) a dispute, which has surpassed the amicable stage must be resolved under dispute-resolution procedures agreed in the contract. Further, both laws allow for the unresolved dispute to be referred to Kazakhstan courts or international arbitration in accordance with the investment legislation of the Republic of Kazakhstan. Of note is the identity of these provisions with the Kazakhstan Law on Investments (Article 9).

MEMR as the licensor on old contracts

MEMR is now clearly instituted with the licensor's functions on the subsoil-use contracts that were concluded prior to the 1999 amendments, which, it is worth mentioning, abolished the licence-and-contract system. The clarified role of the MEMR is essential for administration of subsoil use projects.

Noteworthy changes in tax law concerning subsoil-use operations

From 1 January 2004, the tax regime governing subsoil use operations has changed dramatically. In essence, the state's share in proceeds flowing from oil and gas projects has been increased. Due to the limited reach of this overview, it will suffice here to state that the amendments introduced two model subsoil use contract tax regimes: tax/royalty (known as Model 1) and production sharing agreement (known as Model 2).

Further, for all Model 1 post-January 2004 contracts, tax must be paid in accordance with the tax law in effect at the time the payment obligation accrued. Of note is the introduction of three trigger parameters under Model 2 in the distribution of 'profit oil' share to the contractor, which share is determined as the lowest percentage computed under three triggers: 1) R-Factor (ratio of accumulated income to accumulated expenditures); 2) the IRR-Factor (internal rate of revenue; annual discount rate at which the net present value reaches zero); and 3) the P-Factor (price factor; ratio of income to volume of production over reported period).

Taxation

The Republic of Kazakhstan Code on Taxes and Other Mandatory Payments to the Budget dated 12 June 2001, as amended, regulates taxation in Kazakhstan. The tax consequences of opening a representative office, branch or subsidiary may differ depending on the nature of the activity and the provisions of any double-taxation avoidance treaty between Kazakhstan and the country of the investor. Kazakhstan tax legislation divides foreign legal entities into the following two groups: 1) foreign legal entities acting through a permanent establishment in Kazakhstan (akin to a resident); 2) foreign legal entities acting without a permanent establishment in Kazakhstan (akin to a non-resident).

If the activity of a foreign legal entity does not give rise to a permanent establishment, under Kazakhstan's Tax Code, corporate income tax at a rate of 20 per cent should be withheld at source by the company which pays the income. A non-resident acting without a permanent establishment in Kazakhstan is not allowed to make expense deductions. If the activities do give rise to a permanent establishment, Kazakhstan source corporate income tax should be paid in Kazakhstan directly by such a permanent establishment.

A subsidiary does not constitute a 'permanent establishment' of the parent company for taxation purposes, because it is treated as a separate taxpayer. Under Kazakhstan's Tax Code, the basic rate for the taxation of a subsidiary, like any resident legal entity, is 30 per cent on all income from sources within or outside Kazakhstan. Any dividends paid to shareholders of a subsidiary are subject to 15 per cent tax.

As permanent establishments, branches of non-resident legal entities are also taxed at a rate of 30 per cent on all income from Kazakhstan sources and 15 per cent tax on the net income of the permanent establishment. Kazakhstan tax legislation defines 'net income' as a taxable income minus income tax compounded for this income. Therefore, the 30 per cent tax charge and 15 per cent tax charge have different bases for taxation: 15 per cent tax charge should be calculated from the amount of income after the payment of the 30 per cent tax charge.

As noted above, representative offices are not permitted to engage in commercial activity and, accordingly, do not derive taxable income. Therefore, representative offices are not subject to income tax. In addition, it is possible for foreign investors to be granted limited exemptions from the corporate income tax and property tax under contracts with the authorized body of the Republic of Kazakhstan. Currently, the authorized body is the Investment Committee of the Ministry of Industry and Trade.

All but a few exempt categories of services and imported goods are subject to VAT of 15 per cent; imported capital goods are not exempted. The VAT is paid if the place of the sale of goods (services, works) is Kazakhstan.

Some specified goods, either produced in Kazakhstan or imported, are subject to excise tax. Entities that own land plots in Kazakhstan pay a land tax. Entities in Kazakhstan are also subject to other types of taxes and mandatory duties in certain cases. Entities that own property in Kazakhstan pay a property tax, while entities that own vehicles pay a tax on vehicles. There are also taxes for subsoil users and JSCs for state registration of the share placements.

It should be noted that the taxation of foreign businesses in Kazakhstan is also subject to international treaties, such as bilateral treaties on avoidance of double taxation. By now, Kazakhstan has concluded such treaties with 40 countries including the USA, Canada, France, Germany, Italy, the Netherlands, Switzerland and Turkey.

Arbitration

On 28 December 2004, the Parliament of the Republic of Kazakhstan adopted the Law on Arbitration Courts and the Law on International

Commercial Arbitration (the laws) that set into law general rules for arbitration in Kazakhstan. Below we highlight the main characteristics of both the arbitration courts and summarize the similarities and differences between these two tribunals.

First of all, both of the courts are defined as non-state institutions, where the parties can resolve their dispute as an alternative to doing so in the state courts. Further, the laws establish the jurisdiction of both of the arbitration courts – both can only resolve disputes originated from civil agreements, unless otherwise stipulated by the legislation of Kazakhstan.

At the same time the two laws have defined significant differences between them. Thus, the arbitration courts of the Republic of Kazakhstan cannot resolve disputes related to the state interests, governmental enterprises, juveniles, legally incapable people, activity of natural monopolies and bankruptcy cases. The international arbitration courts, on the other hand, do not seem to be specifically limited in resolving the abovementioned disputes. However, unlike the arbitration courts of the Republic of Kazakhstan, the international arbitration courts can resolve disputes only if one of the parties, as a minimum, is a Kazakh non-resident. Notably, the Law on International Commercial Arbitration does not define the term 'non-resident'. (The Law on Currency Regulation defines this term as all foreign individuals and legal entities, or such Kazakhstan companies, which are not located in the Republic of Kazakhstan.)

In addition, in resolving a dispute, the international arbitration courts may apply provisions of the applicable law agreed by the parties, whereas the arbitration courts of the Republic of Kazakhstan may only apply provisions of Kazakhstan legislation. Also, the laws permit using different languages in the proceedings. Under the international arbitration choice of dispute resolution, the parties may choose any language for the proceedings (if they did not predetermine the language of arbitration, the proceedings can be held in Kazakh or Russian). However, as a general rule, the proceedings in arbitration courts of the Republic of Kazakhstan are held in the Kazakh language, although Russian or another language is not forbidden.

The award of international arbitration courts can be abolished by Kazakhstan state courts upon the request of either party in the event of procedural violations and if the award disagrees with the country's 'public order'. It is worth noting that the award of the Kazakhstan arbitration court can be abolished in the case of violation of the republic's material law. The parties to the dispute and the third parties, whose interests the award in question may concern, have the power to require the award be abolished. Following the abolishment decision, either party may refer the dispute to another arbitration court of the Republic of Kazakhstan, unless the award was abolished on the invalidity of the arbitration clause or arbitration agreement.

Moreover, an important amendment was made to the Kazakhstan Civil Procedural Code with regard to the enforcement of arbitral awards of both international arbitration courts and Kazakhstan arbitration courts. On request of either party or the third party (where an arbitral award was made with respect to a third party), the Kazakhstan court can enforce the award unless there are procedural violations or the enforcement of the award would contradict the public order of the Republic of Kazakhstan.

The awards of the arbitration courts of the Republic of Kazakhstan are enforced in accordance with the Civil Procedural Code of the Republic of

Kazakhstan, which provides for a 'mandatory enforcement of the award'. Upon request of one of the parties, the Kazakhstan court issues an 'enforcement document', whereby the award must be immediately enforced. One has the right to appeal the decision not to issue such 'enforcement document'.

After the issue on either cancellation or enforcement of the international arbitration award has been resolved, the Kazakhstan court issues a ruling, which can be either appealed or protested in accordance with the Civil Procedural Code.

Conclusion

Kazakhstan is in the process of moving from a command- to a market-driven economy. Kazakhstan has actively pursued a programme of economic reform and inward foreign investment designed to establish a free market economy. The recent enactment of many laws, the lack of consensus about the scope, content and pace of economic and political reform, and the rapid evolution of the legal systems in ways that may not always coincide with market developments have resulted in ambiguities, inconsistencies, anomalies and the enactment of laws and regulations without a clear constitutional or legislative basis. Consequently they give rise to investment risks that do not exist in more developed legal systems.

As an overall conclusion, our brief analysis suggests that the continuous development of Kazakhstan legislation requires a higher degree of attention from foreign companies to changes that could have a material adverse effect on the business, financial condition and results of operations in Kazakhstan.

Changes in aspects of Kazakhstan legislation affecting international transaction financing

Salans, Almaty

Introduction

In the course of performing their activities, companies and banks in Kazakhstan actively use finance obtained from foreign and international financial institutions. In this article, we will address certain aspects of Kazakhstan legislation of which international banks should be aware of. This particularly applies to banks that are currently considering the possibility of or are intending to finance international transactions with the participation of Kazakhstan companies or Kazakhstan products.

Although the law of the Republic of Kazakhstan is not a common choice for international transactions on financing, there are certain regulatory aspects of the Kazakhstan legislation which apply to transactions involving Kazakhstan companies or institutions that must be observed. We will look at the most important regulatory provisions of the Kazakhstan legislation for structuring international transactions on financing. In particular, the following topics will be raised:

- currency control issues (including those affected by the new Law on Currency Regulation);
- securing liability of the Kazakhstan borrower;
- antimonopoly legislation provisions in Kazakhstan.

Currency control

Under current legislation major aspects of currency control that are usually relevant to international transactions on financing are registration of transactions with the NBK and obtaining a licence from the NBK for performing such transactions.

For example, according to legislation in effect, loans of value of more than US $100,000 provided by non-residents to residents for a time period exceeding six months are subject to registration. In addition, with regard to international transactions, their structure often requires that Kazakhstan residents open an offshore bank account. Here, it is important to remember that such resident has to obtain a NBK licence in order to open an account.

The new Law on Currency Regulation and Currency Control came into force in December 2005 and has resulted in a number of changes with regard to currency control. The new law was adopted because the previous Law on Currency Regulation (1996) did not address a wide range of transactions and questions that arise in the course of currency regulation and currency control performance in

Kazakhstan. Also, it did not cover some of the aspects of currency regulations, subject to specific rules issued by the NBK. The new law, which is more detailed, contains a number of provisions which were earlier included in the previously mentioned rules. The new Law provides new definitions, including:

- direct investment – which was previously defined in the NBK's Rules for Registration of Currency Operations Relating to Movement of Capital and Opening of Accounts Abroad.
- currency monitoring – carried out by the NBK with regard to branches and the representative offices of non-resident legal entities, which also requires such branches and representative offices to submit reports to the NBK.
- notification regime – presented in addition to the registration and the licensing regimes. The notification regime provides that the NBK be notified of the currency operation and that it issue confirmation of the receipt of such notification.
- financial loan – this definition unified separate or non-existent terms and includes, for example, traditional credits; banking deposits made by foreign affiliates of such banks in order to raise capital on international capital markets; financing of any transactions by third parties.

With regard to the licensing and the registration regimes, the new law provides for softening and\or cancellation of the licensing regime from 1 January 2007 and a shift in the number of the currency operations to the registration and notification regime.

With regard to the financial loans, the registration regime shall remain. It is worth mentioning that the new law does not mention the US $100,000 threshold that applies under the legislation in effect to financial loans, as well as the other currency operations. Presumably, the registration regime under the new law shall apply regardless of the value of a transaction.

Opening bank accounts outside the Republic of Kazakhstan

There is a significant change with regard to the opening of a foreign bank account by resident legal entities. The new law, in some cases, replaces the requirement to obtain a licence with the registration requirement. For instance, it is worth mentioning that a resident legal entity may open an account the registration regime if such an account is opened for the purposes of transfer of the payments in order to secure the liabilities of the residents before non-residents with regard to the loans provided by non-residents.

In addition, the new law provides that from 1 January 2007, the requirement on registration and licensing with regard to opening bank accounts abroad be cancelled. Notification mode shall be applicable to the opening of accounts (with the exception of the opening of accounts by banks).

Securing liability: financial assets security

It's reasonable that any financial institution or bank is interested in providing legal protection and loan security to Kazakh residents. Now we examine the possibilities that Kazakhstan law provides with respect to credit obligations security. Kazakhstan law provides for a rather wide range of legal instruments of obligation fulfillment security, including pledge, warranty, bail and other instruments, which may be provided for in an agreement.

Pledges

First of all it is essential to note that Kazakhstan legislation does not provide for the straightforward transfer of title for assets under pledge to the pledgee. This is in case the debtor fails to meet the obligation secured by pledge. The law stipulates that the claim of the pledgee should be satisfied from the sum of money gained from the sale of assets that are subject to pledge. The sale of such assets may be held in court and/or in out-of-court proceedings, depending on the conditions and terms of agreement.

With respect to the assets, which may be subject to pledge, there are no essential restrictions. In general, any asset and tangible (including immovable property, goods in circulation, subsoil-use rights) can be subject to pledge. However the law prohibits the pledge of: 1)assets, excluded of circulation; 2) claims inseparably linked with the personality of creditor (for instance, a child support claim); or 3) other inalienable rights by virtue of law.

Regarding immovable property pledges, we should note that some categories of land are not subject to pledging. A pledge for immovable property is to be duly registered because it comes into force only from the date of its registration. As a rule, registration of rights over movable property is not required, unless specifically provided for in Kazakhstan Law. Specific cases where the registration of pledges over movable assets is required can be generally divided into two categories. The first category includes cases where a pledge of certain property must be registered and where the relevant registration requirement is directly indicated by law. For example, pledges over securities and vehicles are to be registered. The second category is based on Article 5 of the Law on Registration of Pledges over Movable Property. Under this law, pledges for movable property that are not subject to mandatory state registration must nevertheless be registered if: 1) it is either required by one of the parties to the pledge agreement or to an agreement containing provisions regarding the pledge of the property; or 2) if the pledge agreement or other agreement containing provisions on the pledge prohibits the subsequent pledge of pledged property (ie a negative covenant).

Subsoil use right pledges

Of course, many creditors are interested in creating a pledge over subsoil use rights. Here we note some main issues concerning subsoil use right pledges.

- all field pledges require the consent of the MEMR;
- the enforcement of a field pledge is carried out in the same manner as a pledge of other property in accordance with Kazakhstan law;
- state bodies may not interfere with the sale of a subsoil-use right in out-of-court proceedings;
- the pledge must be issued for providing the subsoil user with money for conducting his subsoil-use activities;
- all the monies, secured by pledge, are be directed for this purpose.

Please note the following aspects of subsoil use right pledges, which can essentially affect the enforcement of pledge. In December 2004, the Parliament of the Republic of Kazakhstan adopted the amendments to the Law On Subsoil and Subsoil Use, according to which the state has a 'pre-emptive right' to acquire the subsoil-use-right and/or the shares of a company holding subsoil use rights under not worse terms and conditions than proposed by other purchasers.

Therefore, while enforcing the pledge of subsoil use rights, it has to be taken into consideration that the state, by virtue of law, has a priority right of purchase over subsoil use rights. Unfortunately, the law does not provide for any specific and clear mechanism for the state to effect its priority right. As a practical matter, we have seen the precedents of compliance with this article of the Subsoil Use Law, where companies apply to the government requesting it waive its pre-emptive right. The government reviews a particular transaction and instructs MEMR to inform the companies on its decision.

Antimonopoly legislation

Obtaining the consent of the antimonopoly agency

In structuring a transaction which envisages acquisition of participation interests of shares in a Kazakhstan company or a so-called 'subject of market', antimonopoly legislation must be taken into consideration. It is worthwhile to consider this provision of law because non-compliance may result in invalidation of a transaction. Article 18 of the Law On Competition and Restriction of Monopoly Activity requires that preliminary consent is obtained from the Competition Protection Committee of the Ministry of Industry and Trade regarding acquisition by a person (or group of persons) of rights. The committee must be allowed to determine the terms for conducting the entrepreneurial activity or to function as an executive body of a company if the total value of its assets (of both the purchaser and the company purchased) exceeds US $700,000.

Obviously, this provision of the law is broad enough so that the majority of transactions on the purchase of shares or participatory interest in a Kazakhstan company is subject to the requirement to obtain preliminary consent of the Committee on Protection of Competition. In general, the procedure for obtaining a consent is quite sophisticated and time consuming. Because of this, many companies may decide not to apply for consent. However, in this case there is a legal risk. From our point of view, this provision of the law is an obstacle to a normal business activity and it is necessary to amend it in order to narrow the scope of its application.

Conclusion

Overall, it could be noted that Kazakhstan legislation provides a rather workable regulatory regime for international financing transactions. Clearly, there is a trend for the liberalization of the currency control regime. However, at the same time there are areas in this regime that might create unnecessary burdens or legal risks for banks and companies involved in international financing.

Amendments to the Law On Labour in the Republic of Kazakhstan

Salans, Almaty

Considerable amendments were introduced to the Republic of Kazakhstan's Law On Labour in the Republic of Kazakhstan (the Labour Law), December 2004. The major changes are described below.

According to amendments, an employer and employee may conclude an individual labour contract for a certain specified period of not less than one year, with the exception of short-term work and labour contracts signed for the period of temporary replacement of an employee. The contract is considered as concluded for an uncertain period if the contract was concluded for the second time with an employee.

New amendments introduced new regulations prohibiting an employer on his/her discretion to cancel the individual labour contract with pregnant women, women with a child or children under the age of 18 months. (Exceptions to this provision are only in cases of employer liquidation, refusal of employee to be transferred to another location within the organization and repeated non-performance of labour liabilities without valid reasons.) In addition, a similar rule was introduced that forbids the employer by his/her own discretion to cancel the individual labour contract with an employee during his/her temporary disability or annual leave, except in the case of liquidation of the organization. According to the amendments, women who have children under the age of 18 months are granted a minimum of 30 minutes paid 'time-out' for feeding, which may be provided every three hours. Additional unpaid child-care leave was extended up to three years.

Under amended Article 26 of the Labour Law, an employer may cancel an individual labour contract if the employee discloses confidential and protected information that became known during the course of his/her work. An employer may cancel a labour contract in the case when employee's right for confidential information is revoked.

The amendments adopted a new definition of 'collective agreement' and 'representatives of the employee', as well as introducing amendments to negotiation procedures, drafting, signing and monitoring of the collective agreement.

An employer now has the right to grant leave for an employee for the first working year regardless of the employee's actual worked time (previously, annual leave was granted only after the completion of one full working year).

Finally, amendments to Article 29 of the Labour Law specify that a reinstated employee (with whom the employer illegally terminated the contract) shall be reimbursed with their average salary for the whole period of enforced leave but for not more than six months (earlier the reimbursement period for forced leave was limited to three months).

Also from GMB Publishing

Ukraine Since the Orange Revolution: A Business and Investment Review

Consultant editor: Dr Marat Terterov

An authoritative progress report on market reforms and the changes to law and commercial practice being instituted by Ukraine's new government, which offers an insider's guide to the current investment climate and the risks and opportunities for foreign investors in Ukraine. It gages the opinions of economic and political analysts, lawyers and the foreign investor community on Ukraine's business and investment environment. The new government's policy objectives included combating corruption and business cronyism, creating a more attractive environment for foreign investment, and moving Ukraine closer to the EU and the WTO. This report reviews progress so far and prospects for the future.

ISBN 1-846730-04-X · 40 pages · Published 2006

Russia During President Putin's Second Term: A Business and Investment Review

Consultant editor: Dr Marat Terterov

Researched and written by lawyers and professional based in the country, this authoritative report considers the latest market reforms and the changes to law and commercial practice in Russia. It covers: recent trends in the Russian investment climate; legal developments and business legislation; changes in the taxation system for 2005-06. It also looks at key trends in Russian business/economic sectors during 2005: energy sector / energy sector legislation; IT and Telecoms; automotive sector; retail; brewing, and at recent mergers and acquisitions. It also includes a special case study: privatization developments in St.Petersburg during 2005. Contributors include Deloitte & Touche; CMS Cameron McKenna; KPMG; Pepeliaev, Goltsblat & Partners.

ISBN 1-846730-08-2 · 40 pages · Published 2006

Turkey: A Business and Investment Review

Consultant editors: Philip Rosenblatt and Dr Marat Terterov

This in-depth report looks at the market reforms and the changes to law and commercial practice being instituted in Turkey as it prepares for EU accession talks.

It assesses the current investment climate and the risks and opportunities for foreign investors in Turkey and provides an invaluable up-to-date guide to commercial law, accounting, taxation, banking and investment and finance regulations. It includes a major contribution from Istanbul law firm Rosenblatt & Co and contributions from Simmons & Simmons, Bee Consulting and many leading Turkish professionals.

ISBN 1-846730-06-6 · 40 pages · Published June 2006

Russian Energy Policy During President Putin's Tenure: Trends and Strategies

Author: Danila Bochkarev

This important report looks at the policies and strategies President Putin has developed in the field of energy and at the current climate for foreign investors in the sector.

Russian energy policy is at an important watershed. A substantial increase in the output of oil & gas, has led some analysts to view Russia as a reliable, alternative to global dependence on energy supplies from the Gulf. On the other hand, there are concerns that current Russian energy strategy comes closer to the Venezuelan 'energy state-capitalism' model where foreign energy companies are welcome to invest, but only on Moscow's terms and in partnership with a state-controlled national energy company. How are these strategies unfolding and what are the lessons for private sector investors?

ISBN 1-846730-26-0 70 pages Published 2006

Renewable Energy in Russia and the CIS

Kevin Smith and Chris Moore

From the authors of Renewable Energy in SEE, this second report looks in the same detail at the RE markets in Russia and the states of the former Soviet Union.

ISBN 184673052X 70 pages Publication March 2007

Russian Foreign Energy Policy: An Analytical Compendium (Volume 1)

Series editor: Dr Kevin Rosner

This important publication brings together a series of authoritative reports, which establish for the first time the confluence of Russian foreign policy with the acquisition of foreign energy assets by Russian entities. Nine specific country profiles focus on the oil, gas, electricity and nuclear power industries. Each report, written by an author of international standing, explains how Russian foreign energy downstream mergers and acquisitions are transpiring to consolidate the new Russian empire.

These unique studies address many questions of substance for energy industry professionals, investors, policy experts, and decision makers who seek to make sense of the dynamic changes that have overcome the Russian energy complex and altered.

ISBN 1846730597 476 pages Publication March 2007

Printed in the United Kingdom
by Lightning Source UK Ltd.
116521UKS00001B/105-108

9 781846 730108